NOT A SOUL WOULD HAVE BELIEVED ME, SO I KEPT QUIET

Sam Braun
Interviewed by Stéphane Guinoiseau

Translated from French by Victoria Taylor

For you Faival, known as Felix, my father.
Murdered in the gas chambers of Auschwitz at the age of fifty-three.

For you Malka, known as Pauline, my mother.
Murdered in the gas chambers of Auschwitz at the age of forty-five.

For you Monique, my little sister.
Murdered in the gas chambers of Auschwitz at the age of eleven.

For you, millions of Jews.
Murdered in the gas chambers of Auschwitz and other death camps.

For you, all victims of intolerance, Jews and non-Jews,
French and other nationalities.
Murdered for believing that all human beings have
the right to live in peace.

May these words be a shroud that you may rest in peace.

Published in 2022 by Real Publishing
www.realfp.com.au

Originally published in French © Editions Albin Michel - Paris 2008

Text © Sam Braun

The moral rights of the author have been asserted.

All rights reserved. No part of this publication may
be reproduced, stored in a retrieval system or transmitted in any form or by any means,
electronic, mechanical, photocopying, recording or otherwise without the prior written
permission of the author. Enquiries should be made to the publisher.

 A catalogue record for this book is available from the National Library of Australia

Images © Braun Family, with the exception of:
page 24 Courtesy of German Federal Archives
page 39 (top and bottom) Courtesy of Yad Vashem
page 50 United States Holocaust Memorial Museum Collection, Gift of Mordecai E. Schwartz
page 111 United States Holocaust Memorial Museum, courtesy of Claudine Cerf
page 121 Shutterstock/Alizada Studios
page 123 (top) Shutterstock/Chris Lawrence Travel, (bottom) Victoria Taylor
page 144 United States Holocaust Memorial Museum, courtesy of Instytut Pamieci Narodowej

ISBN: 9780645213140

Translated into English by Victoria Taylor
Edited by Georgie Raik-Alen
Editorial assistance by Romy Moshinsky
Cover and text design by Anne Stanhope

Contents

Foreword vii

1 From Clermont to Drancy 1

2 Auschwitz-Monowitz 31

3 The Death March, Liberation
   and Return to France 65

4 To Bear Witness 101

5 Return to Auschwitz,
   Forgiveness and Humanism 133

Translator's Note 162

References 164

"To bear witness is to describe what is ultimately indescribable."

G. Didi-Huberman
Images malgré tout
(Images in Spite of All)

"We cannot be prepared for the future without understanding the past."

Germaine Tillion
À la recherche du vrai et du juste
(In the Search for Truth and Justice)

Foreword

In July 1945, a French Army air ambulance landed on the runway at Bourget, north of Paris. A small number of survivors from the Nazi concentration camps disembarked, having been brought home from Prague. After Auschwitz was evacuated on 17 January 1945, they had endured an interminable journey in that seemingly never-ending winter. A journey of murder, death and suffering which had been their final torment before ultimately being left in the Czech capital. For those who survived, it would be several more weeks before they could go home to France. They had to get used to having food again, to having a life again, and to attend to their injuries (the injuries that were visible, that is). They had to try to forget the smell of ash and death.

And so, in July 1945, a young man who was just turning eighteen was coming home. Arrested in Clermont-Ferrand in November 1943, he had spent a short time at Drancy before being deported to Auschwitz that December. Thanks to the exceptional work of Serge Klarsfeld[1] the exact death toll in Auschwitz is now known. Of the 76,000 Jews deported from France between March 1942 and August 1944, less than 2,600 returned. This young man was one of those coming home. But his father Faivel, his mother Malka, and his little sister Monique, who was just eleven years old in 1943, they had all died in the gas chambers on the very day they arrived in Auschwitz.

1. See Serge Klarsfeld, *Vichy-Auschwitz. La «solution finale» et la question juive en France*, Fayard, 1983, 1985. (Vichy-Auschwitz. The Final Solution and the Jewish Question in France).

I picture this frail shadow of a young man, on the summer day of his homecoming to the land of his birth. His vulnerable, intense expression, his tear-stained face. I imagine him as he walked onto the tarmac, his heart gripped by an unspoken sadness but with fresh hope. Then the loneliness. Then the silence. Soon to be shut down by indifference and discomfort. This young man damaged so early by unforeseen grief and the pain of such brutal memories. His name was Sam Braun.

Sixty years later, I would meet him by chance at a conference in the school where I was teaching. Sam came into the library where the conference was to be held. Those gathered, who were making quite a bit of noise just moments before, suddenly went quiet. Sam smiled warmly at his audience. Respectful and unassuming, Sam Braun talked briefly about the circumstances of his arrest, his deportation and his time at Auschwitz. Then for two hours, he talked with his young audience who were captivated by his energy, his clarity and his humanity. There were matters of tolerance, forgiveness, comradeship, anti-Semitism, racism, remembrance and forgetting. Of silence, of history and the value of listening. Everyone who was there that day came away with new-found insights. Once ignited, their interest would not go away any time soon, as shown by the questions and comments from the students in the days following. After the conference, as I walked Sam back to his car, I suggested I record his story so it could be published. I was certain what he had to say should be recorded for future generations. He accepted and we organised several meetings over the next year. I recorded our conversations, and we wrote the work which follows here. Never did his kindness, his patience, nor his generosity falter during hours of interviews.

One day, after several months of our recording sessions, Sam showed me three boxes on a shelf in his bookcase. In them were thousands of letters from young people who had heard him speak.

He let me have a look at them. I was so impressed by the substance and power of their moving, sincere and personal correspondence. I will quote just one letter here, written in 2005.

Dear Mr Braun,

I just had to write to thank you for coming to Senior High School C on 2 May 2005, as part of our Philosophy class with Mr T.

Thank you so much for giving me the most beautiful and moving two hours of my time at high school. I could never have imagined your visit would have moved me so much. Your story was so poignant that I felt I was actually going through the events you told us about. So many times I had tears in my eyes. I was so honoured to meet you and to shake your hand at the end of your talk.

Those two hours have had such a profound effect on me. You have helped me put my life into perspective and I have talked about those two hours with all my friends and family. I thanked Mr T. over and over for giving me the opportunity to meet you.

Thank you so very much.

With my most sincere good wishes,

Yasmina,
Final Year Student (Class 3)

The Holocaust belongs in the past, but it is also a fundamental part of our present. Those years, so far away and yet so near, cast an inescapable shadow over our modern life. In the face of bitterness and emptiness, the humanity that Sam Braun embodies and imparts, dares to believe in the intelligence of humankind and in the possibility of change through education. He looks at the 'banality of evil' together with the stories of the Righteous Among the Nations[2] to reaffirm his trust in humanity. After Auschwitz, and despite Auschwitz.

S.G.

---

[2]. Righteous Among the Nations, or the Righteous are people who, at risk to their own lives, saved the lives of Jews during the Holocaust.

1

From Clermont to Drancy

"For months and months the angst weighed heavily on us all. Every day new racist decrees were proclaimed by the government of Occupied France.

But we children were largely unaware of the tragic happenings around us. We were protected by the defences constructed by our families, onto which crashed waves of horrifying news ... without reaching us."

Jean-Claude Moscovici
Voyage à Pitchipoï
(Journey to Pitchipoï)

From Clermont to Drancy

Stéphane Guinoiseau: *Sam, you were arrested in France in November 1943, with several members of your family, because you were Jewish. At the time you were sixteen years old. You were taken to Drancy, the internment camp in a suburb of Paris. On 7 December 1943, you were then taken to Auschwitz in Convoy No.64. Your little sister, your father and your mother never returned. Before talking in detail about these events, in this first interview I'd like to talk about your childhood, your family and your outlook on life at that time in history. To begin, can you tell us about your parents? Where were they born?*

Sam Braun: My mother was born in Kichinev. Back then it was a town in Russia, now the capital of Moldova.

After horrific events occurred in the town in April 1903, my mother left Kichinev with her parents, her brother and her sister. There had been a terrible pogrom after some minor incident together with some carefully targetted rumours. When I was a little boy, I heard my mother talking about how Jews had been hunted down and murdered in their homes. She told me about the Cossacks throwing Jews to the ground and stabbing their eyes out with their swords. It was an image my mother could never forget. She had been only five years old. The story struck fear in my heart, but I also remember thinking she must have been exaggerating – it just seemed so unbelievable to me.

You can imagine how traumatic that had been for her, just a little girl. What a destiny she had – to practically start her life with scenes of such barbarity, to then end her life in a gas chamber at the age of forty-five. Her life began and ended with barbarity.

After leaving Kichinev she came to France with her parents.

My father was born in Poland, in a village I actually visited five or six years ago. Its name is Novy-Dvor which I think means 'new town' in Polish. It is quite a sad little place consisting of dilapidated little cottages with tin roofs. I went there on a pilgrimage to my father's birthplace, and something very strange happened while I was there.

Can you tell us about it?

Yes. I went to the village with a friend. It must have been in the year 2000. I was then president of a French association that fights extremism, *le Cercle Mémoire et Vigilance* (The Circle of Remembrance and Vigilance). We wanted to create a similar association in Poland.

A French friend who was living in Warsaw organised a driver for us. Another friend, Krzysztof W., an emeritus professor at the University of Warsaw, was our interpreter. With a third friend, who is of Romanian background, we went to Novy-Dvor, about sixty kilometres from Warsaw. After a few navigational setbacks we managed to get there. It was rainy and overcast. My friend Krzysztof asked the first people we came across, people who lived in the village, if there were any Jewish families still living there. Was there a synagogue or any sign that a Jewish community had existed there in the past? "No", one of them replied, "There is nothing left."

Then he asked a policeman. We found out there was still a Jewish cemetery. The policeman told us we should follow the main road, cross the train tracks that went through the middle of the village, take a dirt track on the left and we would reach the cemetery.

The friend who was driving us took a wrong turn and instead of crossing the train tracks, he took a dirt track which was on the left. A little further up in the distance we could see some tombstones. We went a bit closer and then the car got bogged. There was a deluge of rain and the mud and slush were terrible. We got out of the car and trudged through the mud towards the cemetery. I could see crosses on top of some tombstones. I told my friends this could not be the Jewish cemetery because Jews were never buried in a Christian cemetery. It was prohibited by Jewish religious law and the Polish Christians didn't want Jews in their cemeteries.

As I was looking at the cemetery and the crosses, a young man was walking across the train tracks. My friend Krzysztof asked him where the Jewish cemetery was. He pointed to the other side of the tracks, to an area of raised ground of about one hundred metres long and about two or three metres high. I actually thought I could see a tombstone. I just stood and looked at this kind of dug-over cemetery. It was as if the Poles, the Nazis or both, had murdered even the dead of this little village in Poland, erasing any memory of them. At that exact moment, as I stood staring, devastated and sad, at this place where my paternal ancestors should have been resting in peace, a train went past obscuring my view of what remained of the Jewish cemetery. The train consisted of cattle wagons like the ones that had taken me to Auschwitz!

Such an incredible coincidence that couldn't just be a coincidence! I was shocked and appalled, and I wept with a profound sadness. I felt as if the passing train was my father whispering to me, "Go, Sam. That's enough now. You have done all you can. You've come back to the starting point. But stop now. You've come full circle."

You can just imagine the state I was in ... hearing the sound of my father's voice!

After this ordeal we finally managed to reach the Jewish cemetery. It was a sad, forsaken place. Only two miserable tombstones remained, standing all alone. One stood upright rooted in the ground. We could decipher some large Hebrew letters engraved on it. The other tombstone was lying overturned in the dirt. Forgotten by time and humankind.

These two tombstones were the only memorial to the Jews of the village. Two tombstones were all that remained of my paternal ancestors! A no-man's land. A few pitiful, buried remnants swept by the wind and by indifference.

As a keepsake I have two small pebbles on my desk. My friend had picked them up and secretly slipped them into my coat pocket.

As for Kichinev, I never went there.

Your father was of Polish origin and your mother Russian. Why do you think they chose to settle in France?

My father was a great admirer of France. He arrived in France before World War I, and during that war he joined the French forces (as a volunteer because he was still a foreigner).

When I speak of my father I always say that he was so captivated by France he surely thought he had descended from the builders of Versailles! All the bound books you see on these shelves belonged to my father and I can assure you he read them all. He didn't buy books by the metre, as some people used to do to build up their library. He read Victor Hugo, he read Emile Zola, he read Voltaire and he read all the classics, even though he probably didn't speak perfect French when he arrived in France. He also had a profound belief in the Republic, and our country became his homeland, much more so than his native Poland.

In Eastern European countries at that time, Jewish communities lived completely separately from the rest of the country in which they were 'domiciled'. In Poland, and in a large part of Eastern Europe, things were never rosy for the Jews. In certain regions Jews were not allowed to live in the towns or cities. They sometimes came into the towns to work but they had to live in villages reserved for Jews, the *shtetls*.

Did your parents meet in France?

Yes, they were married on 23 January 1920, in the town hall of the

11th *arrondissement*³ in Paris. Together, they both became citizens in 1924.

They settled in Paris?

I think it was in Montreuil near Paris, but I am not sure.

You were born in Paris. Do you remember your time in Paris?

Indeed, I was born in Paris in 1927. I am an old man now! We left Paris for Clermont-Ferrand before the war, in 1937 or 1938, I can't remember exactly. I was a member of the Cub Scouts at the time, it was the youngest group of Jewish scouts in France. I went to the local school in Boileau Street. I went on to La Fontaine Street School in the 16th *arrondissement* before going to Falguière Street in the 15th *arrondissement*. The school still exists, with its school for boys on one side of the street and the girls' school on the other side. At that time there was no co-education in public schools. I have happy memories of my childhood.

Your earliest memories are of Paris?

Yes, they are of Paris. But what are my earliest memories? It's hard to say ... I have flashes, like photos, frozen. There are a few images I still see clearly – like us all leaving to go on holidays with my parents to Saint-Aubin in Normandy. I still have photos from when I was quite young. I had a dark red, woollen bathing suit my mother knitted for me. It was terribly itchy and scratchy. I complained loudly and told her it was itchy but I had to wear it nevertheless. Mum thought I was only acting up and I just didn't like the bathing suit!

---

3. Paris is divided into 20 *arrondissements* or districts.

I also remember *Guignol*.⁴ A little theatre was set up on the beach and the children sat in a circle on the sand. I remember we rented a bathing box which you could do in those days. The bathing boxes were made of wood with wooden wheels as well. There were men who we'd call 'beach attendants' these days. They used horses to bring the bathing boxes down to the water's edge at low tide and then bring them back up the beach at high tide. It was amazing; we kids had so much fun. As soon as the bathing box was in place we would bury its wheels in the sand. I have a few faded photos of that time. But when I look at them now it feels like I am looking at another era. A time so far away it's as if I haven't even been there. Time is indefinable but it also feels that my life has been so short! I feel like that little kid on the beach isn't actually me.

Images of my schooldays, of my life in the Scouts, bring back vivid memories. They still remain with me. I remember a teacher, a master as we called them in those days, who didn't like me at all. Was he anti-Semitic? I don't know. But what I do remember is him making me kneel for the whole morning on a metal ruler on the platform at the front of class, just for having purple ink on my fingers.

What were your parents doing before the war?

Like many people without an education my father was a 'merchant', as they called it in those days. He was a businessman but I don't think he was a very good one. After he had a shop in the Village Suisse⁵, which was in fact owned by the Rothschilds, he launched quite a big business endeavour in Paris in the Rue de Rennes, but then he went broke. My father was probably like me,

---

4. *Guignol* is a puppet show, taking its name from the main character.
5. Village Suisse is a pedestrian shopping precinct established in the 15th *arrondissement* (district) of Paris in 1900. Most shops sell antiques, furniture, interiors and art.

The beach at Saint Aubin where Sam and his family used to go on holidays.

Rue de Rennes in Paris where Sam's father had a shop. Rue de Rennes is a major shopping street in the 6th arrondissement.

business was not his thing. After those difficulties we went to Clermont-Ferrand where he took up an opportunity to open another shop. That was working quite well for the short time it was operating, but then the war came and everything was disrupted.

Do you still have clear recollections of that time in Clermont-Ferrand?

Oh yes!

Did you like Clermont-Ferrand as a city?

I couldn't really say that. Nowadays young people can go out, often alone, roaming the streets so they are really familiar with them. They can become a real part of their city. In those days it was different, at least in my family. We were quite sheltered. My father was quite strict, sometimes even harsh. Did I have any close friends in Clermont-Ferrand at that time before my arrest? I can't say I did. However, I do remember friends at the Blaise-Pascal High School until year 11, friends I have seen again since.

How would you describe your relationship with your parents at that time?

Wonderful! But that is in the context of the times. I had marvellous parents. They were very loving and the family was very important to them. I do believe my father wasn't always faithful to his marriage vows but it never jeopardised the family. He really loved my mother, just as he loved the four of us. It was a little surreal, my father still believed in the eighteenth century idea that it was no big deal for people to have affairs. Also, he was very stylish, with such charm.

So you had quite a sheltered adolescence?

Absolutely! I was indulged by a mother who was an absolutely wonderful Jewish mother. There are two types of Jewish mothers. The Jewish mother who is interfering, possessive and convinced that her children are there just to fulfill her needs. I think that sort of mother only has children so they can be like robots, unquestioningly devoted to their mother.

My mum was nothing like that! She belonged to the second type of Jewish mother: delightful, very sweet, very affectionate and very loving. Maybe I am looking back through rose-coloured glasses, idealising her a little, but I don't think I am far off.

My father was also very affectionate but with less tenderness. He was much stricter. He just reflected more rigid attitudes to bringing up children from that era. At the table we were not allowed to ask for anything we wanted or even needed. We were not allowed to speak. If we put our elbow on the table, our father would pick up his knife (with the blade in his hand, of course) and with the handle ... bang! He would hit us on the elbow. It really hurt! That was to teach us not to put our elbows on the table because it was considered to be bad manners.

I didn't raise my children like that. Obviously they were allowed to speak at the table. In fact, they had a tendency to talk way too much!

In your family did being Jewish mean you had religious traditions, a special culture? At that time did you feel you had a Jewish culture?

You are asking me several questions at once! I felt I belonged to something that was called Judaism but I didn't really know what that meant. I don't remember ever entering a synagogue with my parents, not even once. Maybe I went for a wedding or some other ceremony ... I'm not sure, I don't remember.

Sam with his mother, his little sister Monique, and his father.

My father was very liberal in the real sense of the word. He wasn't a practising Jew and we never followed any religious rituals or ceremonies. One of my father's brothers, David, was a rabbi. He must have sliced all the little willies of the Right Bank of Paris! He was well-known in Jewish circles. He was a marvellous person, very cultured. I liked him a lot.

When my father went to see his brother, he took a sandwich with him. Not just any sandwich, a ham sandwich! He did that just to annoy David and to be cheeky because they adored each other.

Nevertheless, was there a kind of community spirit?

There was probably a sense of community since a lot of my parents' friends were Jewish. But if I felt Jewish without knowing exactly what that meant, it was no accident.

Later, long after liberation and my return to France, I lived my Judaism as a culture, not as a religion. I do not believe in God, a God who asks that we observe rituals which are essentially pagan, not spiritual. I cannot believe in a God who I imagine hiding up behind the clouds, dividing them once a century to look down on his creations. A God who then quickly closes the clouds up again so he doesn't have to look at what disappoints him so much! How can one identify with a culture without believing in God, when the existence of God is at the very core of that culture? Now the concept is clear to me, but at sixteen years of age it was not. I was just Jewish, that was it.

My father gave me much more than religious beliefs. He taught me to love others without expecting anything in return. He showed me to reject any form of violence and to stand up in the face of evil.

As an example, in my family anything that could kill was forbidden, even in a game. We didn't have toy soldiers or guns as other children did. I recall one incident which had really affected me. On my way home from a Christmas party at the school in Rue Falguière, I dropped in on my father at his shop in Rue de Rennes. I had a toy gun that fired arrows, little wooden arrows with rubber tips. My father flew into a rage. I had been so proud of that toy from the Christmas tree at school. For me it was a real trophy! But he was furious and he refused to even look at his son who had something that could kill, although it was just a toy. This upbringing remained so entrenched in me that I oppose all violence and I am a great admirer of Mahatma Gandhi and Pastor Martin Luther King.

So, you were in Clermont-Ferrand when war was declared. What did you know about the war at that time? Had you been actively following events or were you more absorbed in your studies?

I was twelve years old which in those days did not mean having the maturity adolescents have these days. I remember my father hunched over his radio listening to the news. I remember him talking about the Maginot Line – for me it meant very little. We left for our holidays – it was perhaps just before the war – and near Riom-ès-Montagnes I saw truckloads of Spanish refugees passing by. I was shocked by these people asking us for food in a language I didn't understand. Haggard men, together with women and children, in trucks covered with tarpaulins. I can still see them now. I still feel the same distress I felt then, as they looked at us, those hounded men. Was it a premonition of what was going to happen to me a few years later?

I remember my father sitting over his radio, talking about what he had heard, especially messages such as, "Our forces have retreated to their former position." It was a kind of refrain of the time, so that those at home didn't lose hope. My father was really

Sam (right) with a friend before the war.

upset by how quickly the debacle had unfolded in France.

Then, very quickly, Pétain proclaimed himself the 'Saviour of France'. He organised for pink vitamin lozenges to be handed out to all the kids as they sang *Maréchel, nous voilà*[6] in the schoolyard of Blaise-Pascale High (at that time we went to high school from our sixth year of schooling). Every morning we sang this hymn to Pétain's glory and they gave us these lozenges to suck on. They had quite a nice, sharp taste.

What did you know about the Vichy regime at that time? How did you feel about it? Did you have any concerns about the regime?

No, not really, at least not in my case. The relationships I had with my friends who knew I was Jewish didn't change. At school, I never heard, ever, anything that was even slightly anti-Semitic from my friends or my teachers. There was even a female Maths teacher, who I was really quite in love with (that's why I was always top of the maths class!) ... she actually suggested to my father that she could shelter his youngest two children – my little sister and me.

Did you hear of any anti-Semitic decrees?

Not at all. I was living in a bubble.

You knew nothing of the Vél' d'Hiv'[7] *round-up in July '42, or the other round-ups in August '42?*

I wasn't aware of anything. But don't forget I was in Clermont-Ferrand, in the so-called Free Zone, not in Paris which was the real

---

6. A nationalist song written in 1941 by the Vichy regime to show support for Pétain.
7. *Vél' d'Hiv'* is an abbreviation for *Vélodrome d'Hiver*, the indoor velodrome in Paris to which many Jews were forcibly taken after round-ups (mass arrests) by French police in July 1942. Following the round-ups most of those detained were transported to concentration camps.

centre of the round-ups. However, I did hear about the arrest of some University of Strasbourg students who had relocated to Clermont-Ferrand. I cannot tell you the date, but there was a raid to try to track down members of the Resistance from the university. But I didn't know what happened after the arrests.

Do you think your family had the same feeling about what was happening at the time? Did they feel threatened? Do you remember any new concerns or a change in the atmosphere?

In my mother's case, I don't know. My father was very aware of what was going on. But he said he would never be arrested because he was French and he'd been in the French forces in World War I.

We had a cousin, Jacques, who was a little younger than me. He lived with us for a year. His father had been arrested in their apartment in Paris. His mother and brothers had left for the South, then the so-called Free Zone, Jacques was living with us. A month before our arrest his older brother came to get him. My father didn't want Jacques to leave because he was convinced Jacques was safe with us and there was absolutely no risk. Very wisely, the brother wouldn't listen and it was fortunate he took Jacques with him to join their mother. It was a good thing he took him.

My father was sure we were in no danger, given what he'd done in the last war. He was a French citizen who had chosen and loved this country and its culture. His family had never had any trouble. He had actually been warned about our arrest. A friend of my older sister knew a member of the Milice[8] who was in fact a double agent for the Resistance. He warned this friend that we were going

---

8. The Milice was a paramilitary organisation set up during World War II to fight the French Resistance. They later worked for the Nazis in Occupied France.

to be arrested, but when my father was told he refused to believe it. The friend insisted it was true. But in vain.

To reassure my mother we all slept at a friend of my parents' place for three nights. But during the day my father went to his shop, my sister went to her community school and I went to my high school. It was a stupid, useless and quite laughable way to hide! Was I worried? I don't think so – it was all becoming a bit like the treasure hunts I used to play with my friends at Scouts. After three days, as nothing unusual had happened, my father reassured us and we went back home. At 6am the next day the French Milice arrived!

Can you tell us if the German Occupation changed your day-to-day life before your arrest? The Germans invaded the Free Zone in November 1942, one year before your family's arrest. Did having soldiers around affect your daily lives in any way?

I was not really aware of any significant presence. However, my father had to have a 'manager', an 'administrator', a guy who managed the assets of Jews (meaning he took the little money my father had)!

We were on the official lists of Jews. I remember from 1940, all Jews had to 'declare themselves' to the police. I can still see the six of us queuing up in single file at the doors of the police station where our ID cards were stamped "Jew" in red letters inside a square.

It seems crazy now, but the Jews, especially my father, were law-abiding and as it was the law, they complied. One day my youngest son asked me if I resented that my father had been so thoughtless and had done nothing to hide us. Quite honestly the thought has never entered my head. Even if it might seem to have been irresponsible, there was such purity in the love and trust he had for France, which I admire. Even though it may seem thoughtless in light of what happened to us. But who could have imagined the unimaginable? Who would have thought, in the twentieth century, human beings could be murdered so brutally? To contemplate that a civilised state would try to wipe a group of people from the face of the earth!

Do you remember any particular anti-Jewish laws? I don't think Jews had to wear the yellow star at that time?

That's right, we didn't wear the yellow star in Clermont-Ferrand, in the so-called Free Zone. I don't remember if shops were marked to show that they belonged to Jews, I can't tell you. I don't remember any places where there were signs "No Jews Allowed", like some places in Paris. I don't remember Jewish children being forbidden from entering public gardens or sandpits being off-limits for little kids. There was a public garden just opposite our apartment and I could go there without any problem at all.

Such measures victimising Jews did not yet exist in Clermont-Ferrand. Did they come in later? I don't know.

Were there any such measures or was there any particularly different atmosphere at Blaise-Pascale High School?

To my knowledge no special steps were taken against Jewish students, at least in terms of any rules or administrative regulations.

Were you ever the target of any anti-Semitism?

No, I never felt any anti-Semitism at all. That was my experience, but there may have been other Jewish students who complained of overt anti-Semitism on the part of certain teachers or students.

A studio portrait of Sam in his youth.

Had you heard about 'collaboration' and 'resistance' before November 1943?

Yes, but the Vichy government announcements instead used the term 'terrorists' when they talked about members of the Resistance. Yes, I had heard of the Resistance, but I cannot say I had anything to do with it. You couldn't go into the Resistance just like you go into a room ... just open the door and go in! There had to be a confluence of events to be invited to join because everyone suspected everyone else. This was not without reason, as there were so many betrayals and denouncements, and not just of Jews. Some people vented their hatred by informing on their neighbours, their superiors at work, sometimes even people who had been their friends. Human beings are not always admirable!

On 11 November 1943, the night before our arrest, I went to the Place de Jaude, the main square in Clermont-Ferrand which was quite close to our apartment. I went with some school friends and students from the University of Strasbourg. The students were calmly walking around the square beating the ground with two poles. My father was furious at my thoughtlessness. I must say I was completely unaware of the risks. The two poles represented de Gaulle (*deux gaules*[9] means two poles)! It was 11 November and that was how we were observing the date!

It was not any act of courage on my part, I wasn't aware of the danger. For me it was just a game. Did that annoy them so much that they started the arrests? I don't know. But the next morning, 12 November 1943, the Milice came to arrest us and all hell on earth began for my family.

---

9. The pronunciation of *deux gaules* (two poles) sounds the same as de Gaulle, the name of the leader of the Free French Forces during World War II. After Liberation, de Gaulle was head of the provisional French government and subsequently became France's first post-war president.

Sam Braun

So how did the arrest of your family happen that 12 November?

We were living in an apartment on the first floor with a door opening onto a mezzanine. On 12 November 1943 the Milice came at 6.30 in the morning to arrest my father. When they arrived he tried to escape through the door to the mezzanine but they were waiting there too. They unceremoniously arrested him on the spot.

There were five or six of them. All dressed the same in a heavy coat and a hat. When they saw that it wasn't just my father in the apartment, but also my mother, my grandmother, my little sister who was ten-and-a-half, and me, a sixteen-year-old, the guy in charge decided to load us all. I say 'load' because that's the word he used. I don't remember his face any more, but his harsh, contemptuous and hateful voice still reverberates in my head. He had been ordered to arrest my father and it was his decision alone to take all of us. My grandmother was bedridden and could not get up, so he left her alone in the apartment. She probably died there alone and abandoned, because they then put seals on the door.

We had a housekeeper, Suzanne, who I really liked. She was not arrested with us because they knew she wasn't Jewish. This wonderful woman, without a moment's thought, showed such courage. Suzanne knew my older sister was coming to visit us, and there was a Milice officer still watching our place so they could arrest the two older children as well. Suzanne waited outside on the footpath, pacing up and down. My brother was part of a paramilitary youth group at the time, which the Milice must not have known about. When Suzanne saw my sister coming she signalled to her to get away. As my sister later told the story, when she saw Suzanne signal she immediately realised what was happening and she got out of there. If Suzanne was still on this earth she would definitely deserve a medal of the Righteous Among the Nations!

As for the four of us, the Milice officers took us to the headquarters of the 92nd infantry regiment which had been transformed into a prison.

At the time did you know who the Milice were?

Yes. We knew who they were because they were often marching in the streets with their Basque berets! They went around in black Citroën jeeps. They were easy to spot, practically all dressed the same – a civilian uniform with a hat and a black trench coat, often in leather.

Were they of any particular concern?

I wasn't aware of any. I knew they supported Marshal Pétain, and in my family we were not particularly fond of him!

At the time of your arrest, did you think you would stay in custody and then be taken to Paris? Were you really scared or were you quite hopeful?

I was definitely afraid but it was quite impossible to know what was going to happen to us. I was really scared, I felt like we were in another world. In one fell swoop I was plunged into an unknown world of adults. Until then, I'd really only been with teenagers, with my friends from school. Until that day I had lived in a protective bubble created by my parents. Suddenly I was in another bubble, a surreal one.

    The feeling of being plunged into another world was really frightening, but it was like someone else was living and feeling that fear. From the beginning I felt a kind of schizophrenia. Imprisoned. Suddenly being thrown into an alien world, it didn't feel like it was really happening. It was a very rare experience. It was like I was projected into a movie in which I was both an actor and

Sam Braun

Members of the Milice on parade. The Milice was a French paramilitary organisation that worked for the Nazis and the Vichy regime.

a viewer. I was almost split in two. I felt like that from the moment it all began. This unimaginable world became my reality.

Do you still have memories of that prison in Clermont-Ferrand?

Yes, we were not in a little cell, we were in a large room with other detainees and some members of the Resistance. There weren't any other Jews. In the prison I had this terrible fear in the pit of my stomach. It made it hard to breathe and it gripped me like a vice.

When people came back from being interrogated they were covered in blood from having been tortured. The Milice threw them back in the room like they were hurling bundles of blood-stained laundry. I was afraid my father would come back in the same state when he was taken away for interrogation. The image of my tortured father, covered in blood, remained until he came back. Luckily he had not been bashed, at least not in that way, because he had nothing to tell them, other than his Jewish origins!

I remember a tall blond guy with a thick Northern French accent. His hands were handcuffed behind his back, and the metal cuffs were so tight that blood oozed from his wrists. I was so impressed by this man with the strong Northern accent, and he taught me a lot about the meaning of courage. I often think about him. Without doubt he died there. When he came back from the interrogations he couldn't do anything for himself because his arms were cuffed behind his back. So my mother fed him, and after each spoonful he sang lullabies. Can you imagine? This man covered in blood, suffering a thousand deaths, singing lullabies. Maybe he was thinking of a child he'd left at home, or of a child he wished he'd had. I wept with sadness. Sorrow often goes hand-in-hand with horror. To see this courageous man singing lullabies while death encircled him. It was astounding and terrible. I remember the first two verses of one of the laments that came weakly from his swollen lips, "Sweet little man, you are crying. I feel your sorrow..." The melody has never left me and I sometimes find myself humming it in my mind. Incredible!

We ended up staying in that prison for two weeks.

And after the prison, how were you transferred to Drancy?

By train, with two policemen!

Do you remember anything particular about that journey?

Yes, I do. In the prison, when my father was taken to be interrogated, I saw anguish and terror. In the train I saw stupidity! Stupidity that causes harm, stupidity that causes pain, stupidity that assaults the dignity of others.

Like some dreadful criminals, we were guarded by two French policemen in a third class compartment. At that time the trains had three classes. The seats were wooden. The trip from Clermont-Ferrand was long, it took at least nine hours. The two policemen were at the end of the compartment to prevent us from getting out. They were eating sandwiches. The image remains fixed in my memory.

My father, who felt completely French, tried to talk to the policemen, politely, calmly, without the slightest aggression. They did not answer him. I was sitting on my wooden seat, watching them eat their sandwiches and I could not understand. I could not understand why they didn't answer my father who showed them no malice and who was speaking the same language as them. My father was not accusing them of anything. He was just trying to get some information. At least they could have told him they had to guard us until we got to Drancy. No, nothing. They said nothing.

In that compartment it was the first time I felt the appalling emptiness of dehumanisation. For those two policemen, intoxicated by Vichy propaganda, we were no longer ordinary human beings because in their eyes, we were not. We were Jews. So why would they speak to my father when he was different to them?

After that, during all my time in the concentration camp, I knew what it was to be considered sub-human, the *Untermensch* of the Nazis. It was in the train that I had that bizarre feeling for the first time.

There was one occasion when I wanted to go to the toilet. I asked permission. One of the two policemen came with me to the end of the carriage and put his foot in the toilet door so it wouldn't close. Was he worried I might escape down the tiny hole of the toilet seat? I was hurt, ashamed and embarrassed. I was humiliated. I am not sure if he did it out of malice. He was told to do it, so he did it. Without thinking. Such idiocy is dangerous because it impacts people in the most intimate way.

Sometimes students say to me that in the Nazis' eyes we were animals. I say no, because animals have some kind of status, like pets or stock that belong to someone. Whilst we, we were nothing, we belonged to no-one. A cat is a cat and is seen as such. A dog is seen as a dog. We, we were nothing. And I quickly discovered that fact, face-to-face with these men who were French, just as we were French.

Do you remember the arrival at Drancy?

Not at all.

And the days that followed?

Very little. Some images of Drancy come back to me. Frozen images, a little like in dreams. There were these four-storey buildings. I remember that my mother and my little sister slept on the first two floors. My father and I slept on the third and fourth floor. There were no doors and we slept on straw mattresses on the bare floor, like in the prison at Clermont-Ferrand. The buildings were actually constructed by the housing authority but never completed. Someone has since told me, the ultimate irony was that they were intended as housing for the police.

There were no windows. There were no trees or grassy open-space like there is now. There was just dirt. The low-level buildings were arranged in a U-shape and were enclosed by a high fence. I don't understand how some of our fellow French citizens, like the ones who were guarding us, could do the bidding of the occupiers of our country. I have never understood. That's all I really remember of Drancy, other than the hunger, which was worse than in the Clermont prison.

Did the other people in Drancy have any particular fears or concerns? Did they talk about what was going to happen next?

I sometimes heard people talking about 'Pitchipoï' or something like that. But that was all.

Marcel Jabelot, who was at Drancy in October 1943, talked about the anxious wait and the bewilderment of some detained families. No-one could imagine what was going to happen next. He said, "In Drancy, nobody talked about Auschwitz."

Of course! My father, a cultured man, who had always kept up with what was happening in politics, never imagined the danger we were in. Even after Auschwitz it was still so unimaginable, despite all the reports in the press or in the cinema, despite all the graphic photos and reporting.

It also explains why most survivors, of which I am one, kept quiet when we came back.

No, none of us could then possibly imagine the extent of the horror. The barbarity espoused by some men which would be crystallised, systematised and implemented in places that were hell on earth. How could we imagine that a country like Germany could give birth to such cruelties? Even on the train that took us there, my father, my mother, and all the others with us in the wagon could not have known that there, in Upper Selisia[10], gas chambers awaited our arrival. It was completely inconceivable to ordinary human beings.

You stayed at Drancy for a few weeks or just a few days?

A very short time. Just a few days. We left in the convoy of 7 December 1943. We stayed at Drancy, maybe just a week, then we were crammed into a RATP[11] bus to take us to Bobigny station which was right next to Drancy.

The SS were there shouting at us to quickly board the cattle wagons that were lined up along the platform. My parents didn't let my sister and me out of their sight, to keep us with them. Apart from that, I don't remember anything else about our departure.

You left on 7 December in Convoy No.64 which transported about one thousand people.

Exactly one thousand according to Serge Klarsfeld's figures.

When you arrived 661 people were taken directly to the gas chambers and murdered. Another 339 were selected for work, and of those, only fifty would survive. Did you meet any other survivors from that convoy after your return?

---
10. Now South-West Poland.
11. RATP *Régie Autonome des Transports Parisiens* (state-owned train service in Paris).

Never. I have no memory at all of the other people in our wagon. I didn't speak to anyone apart from my little sister and my parents. I was already in my little bubble, trying to shield myself from the reality of that terrible journey. It was as if my soul was escaping an intolerable and unimaginable universe, as if it did not want to be present.

You have talked before about this 'schizophrenic' splitting of yourself in two, which happened when you were first arrested. Do you think it was essentially a protective reaction? Imre Kertész, the Hungarian Nobel Prize winner for Literature, who was deported at the same age as you, talked about a similar experience in Fateless. *The narrator in the novel explains that at times when he was in the camp, he sought refuge in his imagination, or he even looked at his body from the outside and this 'splitting of himself' allowed him to almost keep out the painful awareness of reality, as well as the physical suffering. Some psychoanalysts talk here of a defensive 'cleaving' of the self in traumatic situations.*

No question! From the moment you feel that what is happening to you is happening to another person, this other person who you look at from afar, who is you but not you, then the fear subsides or no longer even exists. I sometimes say I have suffered a lot, but less than I thought, and certainly less than others. This is because I was lucky to be able to isolate myself from reality, to escape from myself. To not live what others are imposing on you, or to use your mind and imagination to take yourself out of a situation, is a form of escape. On that train, I was starting to run away in my own way. To flee in my mind in order to survive.

2

Auschwitz-Monowitz

> "How we feel about our existence depends largely on how others see us. How can one describe the pitiless experience of those who have lived their days as a mere commodity in the eyes of other men."
>
> Primo Levi
> *If This is a Man*

"I have learned there is a part of our personality that is inalienably and perpetually ours and ours alone. It is a fact that, even in captivity, our imagination remains free. For example, I knew how to ensure that while my hands were busy with a bucket or a pick, I always applied the most minimal effort required to do whatever I was doing – for myself, I wasn't there, it's as simple as that ...

... My favourite pastime was, countless times throughout the day, to imagine myself being at home. Constantly, from morning till night, and whenever I could, I always limited myself to the most mundane tasks."

Imre Kertész
Fateless

Auschwitz-Monowitz

We have talked about your arrest and the time at Drancy. You were then taken with your mother, your father and your little sister to the station at Bobigny. From there you left for an unknown destination in a cattle car. What were conditions like on that voyage?

I have a problem calling it a voyage. Although of course, Jorge Semprun called his book about all this *The Long Voyage*! It was essentially just shipping, like one ships objects or animals.

I do not really remember a lot of about it. At first we couldn't really sit down as there were so many of us all squashed in, crammed up against each other like animals. Then, very quickly, in the first few hours, people died, maybe because some people in our wagon were quite old.

Before being in that cattle car, I had never seen anyone die. Death was a taboo subject, it was hidden from children. My maternal grandfather had died before the war. I knew about it but I didn't see his body. I didn't even go with his coffin to the cemetery. So, the dead bodies in that cattle car were, I dare say, the first I had ever seen. It's very strange when you see someone die for the first time. A human being, who just a moment ago had been breathing, moaning and even crying. Yes, it had a strange effect, even when you isolate yourself to escape the nightmare!

The men piled the dead bodies up against the sides of the wagon, just like they were mannequins in a shop! So then we could actually sit down. Towards the end of the journey we were even able to stretch out because so many had died, in our wagon at least. When I think of those three days of suspended reality, I often tell myself that the dead had given us their seat! I didn't know them but I have enormous sadness for them now when I think about their deaths.

I remember the small openings in the wagon with their little black metal bars. There was one on each side and they were so small and narrow that they reminded me of arrow slits[12]. They let in a bit of fresh air, a tiny bit of light and let out some of the smell.

I remember the latrine bucket, it was about a metre tall and quickly filled up. And as the train rattled along on the bumpy tracks a lot of its contents spilled over and soaked into everything – the floor of the wagon, our clothes and even us! I remember the smell, the stench, I should say. The Nazis, intoxicated by their anti-Semitic propaganda, wanted us to become animals. In that train we had indeed become like animals, in appearance at least!

So that was how the Nazi dehumanisation process began.

Despite these horrific conditions my parents tried to distract my little sister and me. They tried to entertain us so the time would pass more quickly. So we would not think too much about the dead. So we could forget, for just a moment or two, the appalling conditions we found ourselves in, and also so we would not think about what was awaiting us.

I am sure my parents could not have imagined what was going to happen to us.

Was there any water or food in the wagon?

No, there was no water and we had hardly anything to eat. I wonder how my father got hold of the little food we had. Some of the babies and old people had probably died of hunger. There were women who wept because they had no more milk to give their children. There were sick people who moaned in pain, before they were forever silent. I will always remember the wailing of the babies. That wailing still sometimes haunts my dreams.

So many writers have written pages and pages about that train.

---

12. Arrow slits are the vertical openings in a fortification or castle tower through which arrows or guns could be fired.

The train I call the 'the train of darkness' because we were at the bottom of an abyss and we could imagine no way out. But no matter how gifted the writers of all those pages, no description can adequately describe the terrifying reality. How can you really describe the look of terror in some people's eyes? How can you really convey the smell that seeped into our beings ... in the wagon that became our prison?

At first, when the SS closed the doors to the wagon, I couldn't make out anything in the darkness. I felt only bodies up against me – unknown bodies. Then, little by little, I adjusted. But, distressingly, I could only make out the people's backs. After some time, I could see my parents and my little sister, and pushing my way through the others I reached their reassuring presence.

Did people in the convoy bring any baggage with them?

Yes, of course. A little suitcase followed us everywhere. We had that suitcase with us in Drancy. When we were sorted during the selection process on the platform at Birkenau, we were told to leave all our bags and bundles on the ground. So my parents put the little suitcase down. We never saw it again, obviously.

What happened when the train stopped and you arrived at Auschwitz?

Firstly, what sticks in my memory is the noise of the sledgehammers, huge sledgehammers, that broke open the locks on the outside of the doors. Then the sliding door of the wagon was violently wrenched open. A rush of cold air assaulted us in the wagon where it had been quite hot as we were all crammed in together. The cold and the explosion of shouting, together with the barking of the dogs, stays with me still. "*Schnell, raus. Schnell!*" They beat us too, to get us out of the train as quickly as possible so the train could go back and get another load of martyrs.

As we got out of the wagons we were beaten with fists, truncheons and rifle butts. There were certainly no steps, we had to jump about a metre to get onto the platform. For my little sister, the other children and me it was easy, even if we were weak with hunger. But for the adults and older people it was more difficult. We had to help them, all while receiving a volley of blows. It was an unbelievable scene.

I remember something else. When we got onto the platform the SS were shouting at us. There were terrified people being beaten with truncheons, women crying and clinging to their children, and children screaming as they were separated from their parents. There were also some emaciated men dressed like convicts in striped clothing. They were already cleaning out the wagons, emptying them of refuse and bringing out the dead which they piled onto handcarts.

We arrived in the afternoon or early evening but it was still daylight. The platform, which historians have called 'the concrete ramp of Auschwitz-Birkenau', is not the one you see when you visit Auschwitz today. In 1944, they built another platform so the victims could walk directly to their execution. But we arrived on the first platform which was relatively far away from the gas chambers.

On the platform there were huge floodlights and a blanket of thick fog which the floodlights could hardly penetrate. The fog was so thick that we couldn't see the beginning or the end of the train. I felt like nature was putting a veil over what was happening there, to hide from the world what was to unfold. I had absolutely no idea what was going to happen to us, none at all. I only felt that there was no going back which made it all feel so unreal. The fog was like a veil of shame, hiding from the world of men something about to be committed by other men.

Then, everything happened very quickly. The women and young children were separated from us. I saw my mother leave on a truck

Auschwitz-Monowitz

Arriving at Auschwitz.

with my little sister. I can still see it so very clearly. It was the last time I saw them. My mother, wearing the pink woollen shawl she had crocheted herself. Standing on the truck, clinging to my little sister, looking straight at me. As for me, I waited on the platform and watched the truck leave with the two of them packed in with the other women and children. My mother held my eyes and her final, lingering gaze stays with me always.

I was holding my father's hand when we were roughly separated by an SS guard who rushed at us from behind. Very quickly, it all happened so quickly. My father was pushed to one side and I to the other. Then he was taken, also on a truck like my mother and Monique.

When I got to the camp I thought I would see the three of them again. Of course I didn't know where they were, but I thought they had gone in the truck because they were older. I was sure I would see them again, there was no question in my mind!

So where were you taken then?

To Auschwitz III. Buna-Monowitz.

What happened when you got to the camp?

When I arrived with the 338 others who had been selected, we immediately had to take off all our clothes. It was very cold, it must have been minus 15 degrees. We stood there for a long time, maybe for two hours, naked in the yard in the open air. I saw the first to die, from the cold no doubt. They fell to the ground, naked. I could not understand.

I was expecting to find my father, my mother and my little sister. Then, I heard some people speaking French not far away from me – some of the men who were wearing the striped outfits. Despite being prohibited from doing so, I went up to them and whispered,

"I came here with my father, my mother and my little sister. Where are they?" Without hesitation one of them replied, pointing to a chimney (it was not actually a crematorium chimney because there wasn't one at Monowitz), "Your family is in there." The same story has been told again and again because so many people got the same answer to that question.

It seemed so absolutely impossible to me, so unreal, that I didn't actually believe it. I thought to myself, "What's he talking about? He's a psycho. Why is he mocking me?" It was shocking, completely bonkers, as we'd say now.

When did you realise that was indeed the unfortunate truth?

The next day. Very quickly. For all the months I was there I knew they had been murdered in the gas chamber that very night.

But still, deep within myself, in my imagination, a small part of me refused to believe the truth. Defying all logic, defying all reason, I told myself it could not be true. What everyone was telling me was lies and I would see my mother and father again. As for my little sister, I didn't have much hope for her. She was too little. The SS didn't keep mouths to feed if they were of no use to them. But I told myself my mother, my father, maybe, just maybe. There was always this 'maybe' deep inside me, living with the certainty that they were among the martyrs of the first night.

So on your arrival you found yourself naked with 338 others of those selected from your convoy. What happened then, before you were absorbed into the rest of the camp and into a squad?

That same night I was shaved, with clippers that lacerated more than they cut hair – on my head, under my arms, my pubic hair. But, despite the shock, I smiled at the shaven heads of some of the others. They looked so ridiculous with their shaven skulls.

Then we had a shower in a room with several shower heads. A few of us had to huddle under each shower head. Did we have any soap? Did they give us towels? I can't remember but I don't think so.

Then I was tattooed like an animal. They tattooed a number on me. The fellow prisoner who had the job of tattooing, roughly grabbed my left forearm, holding it tight against his body. With his other hand he tattooed six numbers on my arm, using a kind of nail stuck on a piece of wood dipped in Indian ink.

I didn't really understand what was going on, but I was no longer Sam Marcel Braun, born in Paris on 25 August 1927. I had become number 167472, born 10 December 1943, there in that corner of shame in Upper Silesia. But I gave in to it and I never really tried to understand what was happening to me. With the tattoo I felt more than ever that I was somewhere else; everything was so unreal. I was totally passive. In any case, what was there to understand? How is it humanly possible to understand that someone could tattoo human beings? Tattooing their arm with a serial number that would become their new identity? What else could I do but submit?

Then we were disinfected with some kind of powder and went through to 'Canada', where other inmates gave us our convict clothes! I'm not sure that I can really call them clothes – a tattered shirt, pants and a 'jacket' made of thin fabric, without any lining, in grey and blue stripes. Or a long striped jacket made of the same really thin fabric, also unlined, which they called a 'coat'. There was also a cap, made from the same fabric and *Mütze* – clogs made from some kind of coarse fabric with wooden soles. So after that, I was shoved into a hut with all the others until the next morning.

I was asked if I had an occupation by one of the detainees who had the job of making lists. I was too young to have an occupation,

I had been in my second last year of school. So he just allocated me to a squad, Squad 55, where I stayed the whole time I was there. It was a squad assigned to construction. During those long months, I sometimes mucked around with cement under the supervision of a civilian. I also worked with a shovel and a pick. If you knew how heavy a pick is and the conditions we endured, you'd realise just how hard the work was!

Monowitz, or Auschwitz III, had been created to use slave labour for the construction of a factory for IG Farben – an enormous German industrial facility that owned many factories. In this location they were supposed to make a synthetic rubber, which I think is called *Buna* in German. The Auschwitz III camp, or Monowitz, quickly got the nickname Buna. Primo Levi (who I didn't know) was also in this camp and he often refered to it as 'la Buna'.

At Buna-Monowitz did you have any knowledge about the existence of other camps? Did you know, for example, Auschwitz-Birkenau and did you know what went on there?

Oh yes! I very quickly found out about that. Everyone was very soon aware of it. The Auschwitz I and Birkenau camps were close to each other, while Buna-Monowitz was about six kilometres from the other two. For various reasons the inmates were often transferred from one camp to another. However, I always stayed in the same camp, always in the same block. The inmates who were transferred to Buna, or who came from another camp in the Auschwitz network, always told us what was going on in the other camps. They were no doubt transferred to meet the organisational requirements of the SS. The SS were very skilled in that area. If they needed needed extra labour they only had to go and get slaves from somewhere else where they were of less use.

What was the worst time of year for the prisoners who had to work outside in such terrible conditions like you did?

The work in Squad 55 was physically really hard. I certainly had times when I was really cold. But I also suffered greatly in the heat because it was very hot in summer. In winter, the arduous work helped me to fight the cold. But sadly it did not stop many people dying of cold. They froze and just crumpled to the ground like rag dolls, their clothes gathered up in a ball. You could hardly distinguish between their skeletal bodies and their tattered rags.

The winter was really harsh and the glacial winds pierced my body under my clothes. But it was also terrible in the summer heat because the work was so hard. Maybe my Russian-Polish origins meant I could bear the cold more easily than the heat? I don't know, but to work like a beast in the heat was really hard for me to bear.

At the time did you know you were building a factory?

Yes, absolutely. How could we not know? The buildings were right before our eyes. It was an enormous factory. I never knew the exact extent of it, but it was huge. There were dozens of buildings. It was obviously a strategic location because we were bombed by the Americans, the Russians and the English. They didn't all have the same bombing techniques, but they were attacking us to frustrate the German war effort.

I later found out not one piece of synthetic rubber actually came out of that factory, which was good to hear. The Allied advance hadn't given the Nazis enough time to produce any rubber.

During the Nuremberg trials, the managers of the factory claimed to have no knowledge of what was happening to us. Who were they kidding? Didn't they see the thousands of prisoners working like slaves? They could easily have recognised us in our striped clothes and our starved bodies. Were we so emaciated that we were invisible? Who did they think they were paying the few marks or pfennings for the work we did, if it wasn't the SS? Historians have actually found proof that IG Farben was paying the SS for our work. Documents exist that clearly demonstrate that.

You talk of the different kinds of bombing attacks – how did you feel? Were you afraid? What did you think would happen?

Strangely, I wasn't afraid. There was a kind of excitement which I later realised was because it made me feel that the Allies knew we still existed. I felt we were not completely alone and forgotten in this world of thugs. The war had not yet finished and the Allies were doing everything in their power to liberate us. Of course, the purpose of the bombings was not to liberate the Buna-Monowitz camp, but that's how I saw it at the time.

During the bombings the inmates stayed outside. The shelters were not for us. Only the SS could go in the shelters and sometimes the kapos[13], as well as the civilians who were working on the construction of the factory, as there were quite a lot of them. Often a bomb would fall quite closeby. About 50 metres, 100 metres. We just threw ourselves on the ground, that's it. Some prisoners were probably killed, but I'm not sure.

When I saw the planes I said to myself, "Go on, boys. Destroy it all." It was a bit like that. When I saw a building destroyed, I felt a kind of pride and satisfaction. Especially when it was a shelter with the SS and civilians inside.

---

13. A kapo was a prisoner in the concentration camp who worked for the Nazis to supervise their fellow prisoners.

Do you remember many bombings?

Yes. From memory there were five or six. Maybe more. The Russians had an amazing technique, very effective. First they sent a plane and the sirens would go off. The SS and the civilians would go down to the shelters. We waited outside until it passed. The Russian plane left without dropping a single bomb. A few minutes later a second plane, again an alarm. That plane also left without a dropping anything. A third plane would arrive. The Germans didn't believe it anymore so they didn't sound the alarm. It was then that the plane dropped their bombs and quickly left. That really amused me.

Now the Americans, they flew very high up in the sky. A first plane would arrive and make a big circle with smoke, well let's say it was a kind of smoke. Then the flying fortresses[14] would fly through the centre of the huge circle of smoke and drop all their bombs in one hit. The bombs fell where they could, not always on buildings, but because they dropped so many bombs at once they could do some damage.

The English bombed with more precision than the Americans, and at a lower altitude.

What was an ordinary day like for a prisoner working in the construction squad?

We got up very early every day at 4am or 5am, depending on the season.

We would have a quick wash without any soap or towel. Then just as quickly, we wolfed down our 'breakfast' – a ladle of dark, tepid, sugarless liquid they called coffee. There was also 200 grams

---

14. B-17 'flying fortresses' were a kind of bomber used by the United States Army Air Corps during World War II.

of bread which was black in the centre and a bit sticky (the bread was so dense that a slice measuring 2cm by 2.5cm would have weighed 200 grams) and there was 15 grams of margarine. Once a week we got a teaspoon of a sort of jam and a slice of sausage that looked like garlic sausage, but sadly didn't taste like it.

We then left the hut and gathered in the yard in the centre of the camp, in the spot assigned to the barracks where we slept. The morning roll call could go on for hours. In this windy corner of Poland the winter was often glacial. We would stand back-to-back to warm ourselves as we remained in our allotted places. The animal warmth of our bodies would pass between us.

When we came out of the barracks we had to bring out anyone who had died in the night, so they could be deducted from the roll call. We were in rows of five, then the roll call would go on and on. They counted us, recounted us and recounted us again. I thought they didn't know how to count, but it was actually just one of the methods they used to dehumanise us. For the SS, we were *Stücke*, just scraps!

Once roll call was over, after they had counted up their slaves, we regrouped into squads in the same yard. Then we left, all the squads one behind the other, always in fives. Leaving the camp we always tried to avoid being on the outside of the rows of men, on the left. On the left side of the column you would get beaten, mainly by the *Arbeitälteste* (the 'work chief'). He counted the members of every squad as we passed by, and he would hit each one of us. On the right side of the rows there was an orchestra! Can you imaging that? Such cruelty! Such depravity! An orchestra of distinguished musicians, prisoners of course, forced to play music. It was unbelievable! Unspeakable brutality blended with music that had been intended to calm the soul!

We went out, marching in step for several hundred metres. We then quickly entered the grounds of the Buna factory. When we came back in the evening it was obviously the opposite. The orchestra was on the left side of the rows of prisoners and the *Arbeitälteste* were on the right. But they still hit us on the head, counting each member of the squads.

When we got back to the central yard we regrouped again, like in the morning, in the spot assigned for each barrack. And just like in the mornings, the roll call went on and on, we were tormented and we were freezing cold. For the last roll call we had to stand completely still without moving.

When the roll call was over we went back to the hut to line up for our meal, some soup – a litre of lukewarm water with a few pieces of potato in it. Well, that was for the ones who came last in the queue, when it got to the bottom of the pot. The ones at the start only got liquid with nothing in it!

So who was controlling you in terms of authority?

Mainly the kapos. On the worksites, depending on the day, only one kapo supervised us after getting his orders from a civilian foreman. As far as I was concerned, I never had much to complain about the foremen. I don't know if they were Polish or German, but whatever they were they spoke German.

And back at the huts? Was it still the kapos?

No! The kapo was done. The management of the concentration camp was two-fold. There was management of the works, and management of the camp which was all done by the prisoners themselves. The work was spread between squads of various sizes.

There were a lot men in my squad, several hundred for sure. The head of the squad was a kapo. The *Arbeitälteste*, also an inmate, was in charge of the work and of all the kapos and all the squads. He was a fat guy, German, a real brute. He was dressed in black and wore a red triangle for a political prisoner. At the same level as the chief of the camp was the *Lagerälteste*, he was also a nasty brute. He was a political prisoner too, with a red triangle. Below him were the heads of the blocks, called the *Blockälteste*.

So there was a duplicated organisation, with a pyramid structure. Each hierarchy was theoretically independent, but they must have all got on really well, as at the end of our barracks there was a door leading to another, smaller part of the block, where the head of the block and the kapos slept. Our bunks, with three levels, were in the central part of the barracks.

What nationality were the kapos?

There were some Germans, some Poles...

As a prisoner did you have anything to do with the other 'triangles' – the political prisoners, common criminals or any others?

In my case I found refuge in my dreams. That's a simplification of course, not completely accurate but I often say that for almost two years I didn't speak. I had hardly anything to do with the other prisoners. My dreams were enough for me, and I lived in almost total silence.

However, I do remember one time when I talked with a guy wearing a green triangle, a common criminal. He told me how to break into somewhere through a door. He explained that he never forced a door with a crowbar on the side of the latch, but on the other side. When he was robbing some place he always forced the door on its hinges. I have to confess I was fascinated. But I think he would have had a problem if there were bolts at several different points. But was it true? Was he also living in his dreams? That's about all! I had almost no contact with the other inmates.

A drawing by a former inmate whose barracks were similar to the ones Sam slept in at Auschwitz.

Auschwitz-Monowitz

Were there any other French prisoners in your squad?

Yes, but not many. There were lots of Poles, Germans and Hungarians. They came to the camp later on, in 1944. Some Romani people also arrived, but they never lasted long.

Was there any sense of community amongst those prisoners? Did they gather together in nationalities?

People like Primo Levi, who was in the same camp as me, have said there was, but I really couldn't say. I don't know. I always kept to myself so I had no contact at all with any prisoners from France.

You didn't feel any sense of solidarity?

Practically none. Although one time, a prisoner gave me some tobacco powder he had spread onto a wet piece of newspaper and then rolled it up. How did he 'organise' that, as we used to say, I don't know. Nor do I know how he got the match to light this pseudo-cigarette. But what I do know is after coughing and spluttering, my hunger diminished for a short time. That was the only time I ever smoked tobacco like that.

So you mainly had the feeling of being completely alone?

Yes, except for one other time when an inmate did something that probably saved my life. It was a Sunday afternoon and we were not going to work. That in itself was quite incredible! Despite their need for manpower, on Sunday afternoons we didn't work!

Block 10, where I slept, was quite close to two other blocks used for the KB, the *Krankenbau* or infirmary. We were separated from the two blocks by barbed wire but it was not electrified. I was on one side of the fence and on the other side there was a prisoner wearing a dirty coat that had once been white. In German he asked me how old I was. I answered him in German as best I could – seventeen. When he realised I was French he started speaking to me in French and asked my registration number and what block I was in.

I don't really know how it happened, I have completely blocked out that time, but the next morning I found myself in the KB. Did the head of the block order this? I can't remember anything about it now. But there I was in the 'infirmary'. The doctor – the guy was a doctor – kept me there for about eight days even though there was nothing wrong with me, other than exhaustion.

It was so incredibly good for me. I didn't have to get up at dawn or go and work at Buna. I walked freely around the infirmary and as soon as any SS was coming I lay down on the nearest bed, even if there was an actual sick patient in it! The doctor was Doctor Robert Waitz, an amazing man who resisted in his own way. He helped me in the same way as he helped all the living dead in that place.

He later became the dean of the Faculty of Medicine in Strasbourg. He was an excellent doctor. A humanitarian. He had saved my life, but I never went to see him later on, when we had both been liberated. It is one of my biggest regrets. But I didn't want to go and see him for fear of reminding him of those terrible times. Or perhaps it was really because I didn't want to talk about it myself at that time.

To have not gone and thanked him, as he deserved, was a kind of cowardice on my part. Perhaps it was also that I didn't want to revive all the memories I had suppressed. Such cowardice, I will never forgive myself; it will weigh on my conscience for the rest of my days.

Was that your only stay in the infirmary?

Yes, my first response is that it was the only time. However, I do remember I also stayed there for a few days once when I had dysentery. But I don't have any distinct memories of that time.

You have spoken about a 'rest' on Sundays. What did you do then?

We wandered around the camp. There were some 'distractions' so there would be no chance for any let up in the dehumanisation process.

Some Sundays there was a visit from the 'Muslims'. I never knew why the SS called them Muslims, they were the inmates considered incapable of work. Maybe it was because with our empty stomachs we walked doubled-over like Muslims at prayer? And because people who could barely go on any longer were even more bent over, so they looked like the long processions of Muslims at Mecca? I don't know. But that's what the SS called this group of people.

We walked passed an SS guard who was sitting on a chair outside the hut. We were naked from the waist up and despite my exhaustion I still had to look strong, or at least strong enough to keep working. So I tried to puff up my pectoral muscles to show I still had it. With his cane, his riding crop, the SS guard would push everyone he thought incapable of working to one side, and let the others pass by. The ones he pushed aside were loaded on to a truck and I knew very well where they would be taken. Everyone knew. They knew it too. Now it seems unbelievable, but on their faces it was as if they were already dead. There was just a sort of look of resignation, or maybe even relief, to realise that soon it would all be over.

There was also an inspection for lice. When the lice were itchy you squashed them and the squashed lice would leave a stain of fresh, red blood. The blood they had just sucked out of us and maybe their blood as well.

We walked in front of an SS guard showing him the inside of the rags we wore as a shirt. He would separate the folds of our clothing with his riding crop. Sometimes, when he saw a fresh blood stain he would push the prisoner to one side.

Then on some Sundays there were hangings. All those who tried to escape, for example, were hanged.

Were you forced to attend the executions?

Yes. All the prisoners were assembled in the yard, and at the end of the yard stood those horrendous gallows.

I remember the final execution. It was in November or December 1944. We could already hear the sound of the guns coming from the Russian front. Primo Levi also tells this story but he only describes one gallows. As I remember it, there were three. I felt like I was at the Mount of Olives, an image like that popped into my head, Jesus and the two thieves. Of course, they were crucified, while these ones were hanged, but that image will never leave me.

The hangings were exactly like something out of a comic strip. The executioner put the noose made of rope around the neck of each victim who was standing on a trapdoor. The condemned stood there with the rope around their neck, waiting for the commandant to arrive – one minute, two minutes, ten minutes maybe. It seemed to take so long! When the commandant arrived he turned towards us, legs spread, standing firm in his shiny boots, glaring at us with a look of dominance. He sometimes patted his dog, as he thought his dog was far more important than us. Then he suddenly turned around and shouted an order. The executioners pulled a rope opening the trapdoor. The poor unfortunate fell into the void. The commandant turned back towards us smiling – just think, he had killed a Jew!

That day, before the commandant had arrived, one of the three condemned prisoners had shouted in German: "Be brave, brothers. We will be the last!" Primo has recounted this gruesome tale in his book, *If This is a Man*.

"Be brave, brothers. We will be the last!" What he said has stayed with me for a long time. It was a great lesson in courage. I find it so admirable that this man, who knew his death was imminent, spent his final moments thinking about others. To give them courage to go on little longer, to not give up hope.

After the executions we had to walk past the victims who stayed there for hours, hanging in the void. After someone has been hanged their tongue sometimes pokes out from their mouth. To me it was like he was poking his tongue out at the executioners, mocking them.

Everyone who talks about the camps says that the hunger was quite unbearable and became a real obsession. Henri Borlant, a survivor who often talks about his experiences, especially to young people, has described it like this, "Hunger was something that completely overwhelmed you. You couldn't think. You couldn't feel. You were just ravenous ..." In the book about Auschwitz, The World of Stone, *by Tadeus Borowski, one of the characters says, "Hunger is when one human being looks at another thinking they could be eaten." Do you have any memories like that, of hunger and thirst dominating the daily lives of the inmates?*

For me, it's quite strange. I suffered from hunger a great deal, like my friends, but I got used to it. I got used to it because of my daydreaming, when I imagined myself devouring food to satisfy my hunger. I am talking about dreaming while I was awake, a conscious imagining, not dreaming when I was asleep.

The food I dreamed about was only ever two things: shepherd's pie, and buttered bread with a milky coffee. The shepherd's pie was because my mother, who was an amazing cook, made a superb shepherd's pie. I have never been able to find anything that could match its aroma or its sublime taste, despite trying to find it in all the bistros of Paris! Mainly because it was my mother's, and then maybe because it only existed in my imagination. I also often dreamed of buttered bread and milky coffee because that was what I used to have for breakfast.

Every time I was really hungry, which was often, I would lose myself in my imagination. I was eating with such physical concentration, with such belief, that I could smell the aromas, so it actually relieved my hunger. At least that's what I felt, so that was the important thing. I reflect on the power of the mind over the body when I think of all that again.

My imaginary meals were able to temporarily relieve my pain. It's extraordinary. Because hunger is like pincers that twist your stomach, a kind of octopus that consumes you from the inside.

What were the conditions where you slept at night?

We slept in three-level bunks on straw mattresses with an awful blanket full of holes and bugs. The conditions were quite unhealthy, to put it mildly!

And you could still sleep?

Yes, it is amazing. I was so exhausted! What's incredible is that at the end of 1944, when the Hungarians and the Romani people came to the camp (although very soon I didn't see the Romani anymore), there were so many people at Buna-Monowitz that five of us were on each level of the bunks. That only lasted a few days but I still managed to sleep.

Apart from sickness did you often suffer from beatings, violence or abuse?

Not often, no. I was lucky to not have got the *schlague* – a series of beatings on the buttocks and kidney area with a rubber truncheon. It was a thick hose which was probably used for high-tension electrical currents because it had a thick metal core inside. They would hit inmates with it. I was lucky not to be beaten with that thing because it was a real weapon, even if it didn't fire bullets! Ten, twenty, thirty, fifty blows which the victim had to count out in a loud voice in German. Often the poor guy could not count to the end and he lost consciousness. Of course I also got beaten sometimes, but lucky for me it was not that kind of beating!

Did the kapos hand out those beatings?

Yes, the kapos, but mainly the *Arbeitälteste*.

In such conditions was it possible to think about escaping or dream of any kind of resistance?

No, I never thought of escaping, I just thought it was not possible.

I was in a really harsh environment in the middle of Poland and I didn't speak the language. I would have needed a wig to hide my shaved head. I would have needed civilian clothes and help on the outside. I had none of those things.

To my knowledge, anyone who tried to escape from Buna was inevitably captured and after being tortured they were hanged.

Were you aware of any hostility from the locals living around the camp?

Not at all. How could I have been aware of that? I had no contact with any locals. But I can imagine there would be hostility, knowing what little affection the Poles had for the Jews.

Many people have described an insidious anti-Semitism in the areas around the camps. And those who did manage to escape would have no doubt been betrayed by local Polish civilians. Claude Lanzmann's film, Shoah, *leaves little doubt about the long-standing, and also present-day, anti-Semitism of some of the villagers.*

My only contact with civilians was with the foremen. I never had any complaints about them, but nor did I see any compassion from them.

I do remember one incident that had a great impact on me. One day in the first few weeks after my arrival, with about thirty other prisoners from my squad, I was assigned to build a concrete wall enclosing a big piece of land of five or six metres square. The walls were very thick, maybe a metre. We were up quite high on some scaffolding and cement would be sent up to us, in little piles, on a circulating, continuous band. We had to pack the cement into trenches marked out with wooden planks. Two prisoners, who were probably exhausted or even dying, fell into the cement. The civilian foreman immediately ordered that the machine be stopped so they could get the two unfortunate men out. But the SS guard who was there ordered that the work continue, and the men's bodies were slowly submerged under the cement. The foreman had had a normal, humane response in wanting to stop the machine to get the guys out.

Another survivor has said, "From time to time, there was a horrible smell." And Jorge Semprun said in an interview, "What defined the camp was the smell of the crematorium ovens." Did that smell also affect you?

Yes, there was a smell but it wasn't the smell of crematorium ovens which I imagine was the smell of burning flesh. At Auschwitz-Monowitz there wasn't any smell like that because there was no crematorium. We were several kilometres from the gas chambers and the chimneys of the crematoria. Actually, what I remember is the smell of the camp itself, a smell of filth – acrid and persistent. It was an awful smell which was very occasionally blown away by the wind.

One thing that struck me was that I never saw a single bird in that place. I love birds, so if I had even seen just one I would have remembered. Maybe the atmosphere of death kept the birds away. It's strange, nevertheless.

What you have described is a world of suffering where humanity is non-existent. Where respect, empathy, compassion and dignity are completely obliterated. In that tragic world, did you ever feel any moments of complete despair and surrender?

I never felt despair in any absolute form. Except the last day. The last day I was begging for death. It was at the end of the Death March, we will talk more about that later.

In the camp I never wanted to die. I never had a feeling of desperation. Never. No doubt I was convinced, deep down, that I would get out of there.

School students often ask me how I was able to stay alive in Buna. I respond that for me, at least, there were three factors.

First of all, it was luck. But this is not really a quantifiable factor.

Then, there was my imagination. It gave me some small escape into a world that was not real, but it was more humane, and this saved me.

And finally, there was hope – in terms of an expectation for a time in the future. This is not to be confused with hope in terms of an assumption. Hope in terms of an assumption is a short-term thing. One hopes to eat well when one is hungry, to sleep well when one goes to sleep. Hope in terms of an expectation is a longer-term thing.

A philosopher has said that hope, in terms of an expectation, is a feminine word in French (*l'espérance*). Whilst hope, in terms of an assumption (*l'éspoir*) is masculine. Being feminine, hope in terms of an expectation means being capable of creating one more hour, like a woman is capable of giving life. This extra hour is then added to another hour, and all the hours become days, the days become weeks, and the weeks become months. In the camp, this kind of hope, a longer-term hope, never left me.

Is there a limit to this kind of longer-term hope? Perhaps, as on that last day I actually did want to die. I could go on no longer.

So what did you feel then when you saw the 'Muslims', the people who had given up any hope, any desire to live?

When I saw those prisoners leaving on the trucks I had a feeling of defiance, not giving up hope. A feeling of defiance because I knew they were heading for a certain death. They were leaving on the trucks knowing exactly where they were going. There was a kind of acceptance in their eyes. As I've told you before, I remember a kind of passivity before the inevitable. An absolute resignation, a complete calm and maybe, for some, a sense of relief.

That is what sometimes surprises young people and that's what leads to some naïve questions. They wonder how people facing a certain death do not resist or make one last desperate attempt to fight back.

In hindsight, I think we were living a kind of fatalism. It was as if the inescapable wheel of destiny could not be stopped and it just crushed us. We were depleted physically and psychologically – our stomachs were too empty. Didn't a philosopher once say that in such situations, in order to liberate yourself you need to have a full stomach?

And death can be a kind of deliverance?

Indeed. That's why on that final day I had chosen death. As a deliverance.

Maybe some of the 'Muslims' told themselves their deliverance had arrived. But it wasn't always like that. There was more a kind of fatalism, surrender and resignation in their eyes. When one has arrived at a state of such physiological misery, weighing almost nothing, one can also no longer weigh anything in one's mind. They were incredibly thin, weak and as emaciated as it is possible for a human body to be.

In a way, the psyche collapses with the physical. The life force is spent.

Yes, I think so. It gets to a point of physiological misery, when the body gives up, the spirit collapses too, and even to think is impossible.

Charlotte Delbo said you couldn't even think in that place. But, if it was impossible to think, I would not have been able to escape into my imagination, which I did all the time. In that way I believe she and I really didn't have the same experience. Or rather, if there comes a time when the physiological suffering is just so great that one can no longer even think, let alone react, I had not really reached that point! My ability to think had not completely gone under, until those final days.

Roger Perelman, also a survivor, explained that for him, thinking meant suffering. Because for him, to think was also to remember things from the past. He tried to avoid thinking because each thought led him to his past life, and the stark contrast with his present was just too painful. This kind of mindset is also understandable. The desire to suppress one's conscious thoughts because they are just too painful. In a way, the desire to turn into stone.

Absolutely. It really depends what you think about. If your thoughts turn to a memory it can lead to despair.

I completely understand what Perelman is trying to say. In a way he is right of course. I will use a more recent term, 'ruminating thoughts'. The kind of thoughts that make you ruminate about what was and what is no longer – a loved one who has died for example, the kind of thoughts which cause immense pain. Looking back can lead to despair.

However, there is also positive thinking – entirely invented and abstract from one's imagination even if it is based on real people.

Do you think there were other factors for survival? Some people have spoken of their faith or their principles for example.

No, I don't think so. Maybe some people got through it because of their belief in God, because some people still believed in God, even after all that.

For me, God died in Auschwitz, as a German philosopher has written. But for others it was probably not the case. Maybe such belief gave people something to cling to, what I call hope. Without doubt their belief gave them hope.

Primo Levi, among others, has said that a knowledge of German was an important factor in survival. He said in his book, If This is a Man, *you had to understand orders and to communicate to get through. How did you cope and what knowledge did you have of German?*

I hadn't studied any German. I really don't know how I managed to understand what was going on. I really can't tell you.

I actually didn't get many orders. There were sirens. You went to the central yard. You went to work. Nobody really said much to me in German. As I didn't really have much to do with anyone else, not understanding German wasn't really a problem for me.

Others have also spoken of personal hygiene as being a survival factor. In If This is a Man, *a person called Steinlauf explained to Primo Levi that keeping clean was really important. Because to look after one's body, apart from the hygienic benefit, also allowed one to maintain some human dignity. Did you feel that?*

Absolutely. Yes, yes, I can say I did everything I could to keep myself clean, as much as was possible. Obviously, I was dirty, just like everyone else. There was no soap and no towels either. I did everything I could to try to keep clean with the little water we could use from the big basin we all crowded around every morning. In the centre of the basin there was a thin dribble of running water, often freezing cold. Yes, I tried to be as clean as possible, or the least dirty as possible. Primo is correct.

Did you come to have any feelings of hatred, contempt or defiance? While you were there, did you even dream of taking revenge on those responsible for all the death?

Strangely enough, never.

How do you explain that? It would be natural to resent your abusers and to want to take immediate revenge, even just in your mind.

I really do not know. Maybe it was how my father raised me, but I have never known hatred.

The desire for revenge, or vengeance, never occurred to me, even while I was in the camp. I never felt any hatred, even for my abusers. What did I feel about them? Maybe contempt. Yes, definitely contempt. But not hatred. I never felt hatred. Even now it's not a feeling I am familiar with.

Mahatma Gandhi, who I really admire, said, "If you take an eye for an eye, the world will be blind." I want only to open people's eyes, not intensify their blindness or their indifference to injustice.

When you take revenge it actually brings no satisfaction, no fulfillment, no peace, in fact it is the opposite. I would also add that even when faced with the unbearable pain of the murder of my parents and my little sister ... to think of committing the same barbaric act, the same inhumane acts carried out by their murderers, I could never be proud to have those feelings.

After talking about the first impulse for revenge, another survivor, Joseph Bialot, also writes in C'est en hiver que les jours rallongent[15]*, "After we came back I often wondered if we survivors had failed. I thought we should have become killers. For each death, there should be another death. For each murdered child, another murdered child. For each tortured person, torture another. For each despair, another despair. But the price for that may have been to sleep without dreams. If we had done that we would have handed the SS their victory. We would have become just like them.*

I absolutely agree with that final observation. We would then also become murderers and we would have lost our humanity.

The Nazis wanted to rob us of our humanity so we became 'non-humans'. If I had hated the SS, I would have returned in a permanent state of hatred (as some people did, unfortunately) full of bitterness, revenge, vengeance – then the only winner would be the torturer or the murderer.

I think I might be flattering myself in a way, but as far as I am concerned, despite everything I went through, I came out as the winner from this horrific experience. With me, the torturers lost.

---

15. At the time of writing, this book by Joseph Bialot has not been translated into English. The title means: In winter the days got longer.

Do you feel the extreme experience you went through in the camps taught you anything about human nature? Could it have had some anthropological value?

Definitely. We are never free of the past.

Our future is written with what we have experienced. That is to say, what we will become and how we will be is, in a way, a reflection of our past, imbued with its sometimes haunting presence. This can be really negative. Some former prisoners continue to live as though they are still in the camp. They are still living what they suffered in the camp. They live it and relive it, to the point that they endlessly dwell on their time there, with all the psychological danger that poses for their children. They replay it over and over, and talk about it to their family, to their children, to their friends and between themselves whenever they meet up. But I feel sorry for those people more than I blame them. Because how can they ever be happy being like that? Can you even have a life when your memories are infested by such a past? These people who remain in a permanent state of hatred and rumination, never leave the camp.

Others, like me, can say they learned things there, but unfortunately such learning is not quantifiable. As I often joke to the students, "To be able to quantify exactly what I learned there, I would have to live two lives. One with Auschwitz and one without, so I could compare the two!"

What I do know is that I learned tolerance, respect for others, the value of life and hope. I learned that life is a priceless gift and should not be wasted. That human beings should do all they can to achieve something.

I learned that to achieve something in one's life is to not follow the crowd, not to seek power at all costs, because the quest for power is never satisfied, it is never-ending and exhausting!

I have learned that to achieve something in one's life is to be able to look back at your life and feel it has been positive. That you have accomplished more things you are proud of, than you regret.

I have also known, in my body and soul, the horrors of racism and anti-Semitism. I have learned of the injustice of rejecting another because of their appearance. I have learned to respect the dignity of all human beings, even my greatest enemy. I have learned, as Gandhi said, "Each human being is light and shadow", and if we are not careful we are all capable, one day, of becoming the tormentor of another, in our family, or in our work life.

Of course I would have preferred to have learned all this in a different way, because sorrow is not redemption. Certainly not! At least I don't think so. But as this sorrow was imposed on me, I try to get something out of it, to learn from it. In my life I have tried to do as Sartre said, "You should not think about what was done to you, but what you have done with what was done to you."

3

The Death March, Liberation and Return to France

> "I am leaving Auschwitz yet I feel no joy, only great loathing mixed with a vague feeling of triumph. I have won the war. I am alive. That's all.
>
> ... To be freed does not mean to be free."
>
> Joseph Bialot
> *C'est en hiver que les jours rallongent*
> (In Winter the Days got Longer)

> "In any testimony we must always work to disentangle the absurd brought about by terror."
>
> Régine Waintrater
> *Sortir du génocide*
> (Coming Out of Genocide)

We will now turn to the year 1944 and talk about the circumstances of your liberation. What were conditions like in the final weeks before the evacuation of Auschwitz in January 1944?

My first memory of that time, at least what I still remember, vividly, is the sound of the guns. In fact, it still arouses such strong feelings to this day. The Russian-German front was approaching Upper Selisia, where Auschwitz was located, and I could hear the bombing. Were the guns Russian or German? Probably both, but for me they could only be Russian, and as the explosions got louder I felt liberation was coming. The German forces seemed to be so weakened that the shelling could only be, to my way of thinking, shelling by the Allied forces. I think I heard them from November, maybe even October, but I cannot be sure of the exact timing.

But what I do remember is that when the wind blew in our direction, I thought the front was approaching the camp, and my deliverance was at hand. But the sound of the guns was weaker when the wind changed, turning in the other direction. The front then seemed to be withdrawing, and the moment of my liberation was further away. So it was quite disheartening and a blow to our morale.

From then on there weren't any more hangings. There were also no more really violent episodes on the part of the SS, no more vicious attacks where someone was beaten to death, for example. Before that, killing a prisoner, especially a Jew, seemed to be completely banal to them. But if the SS had become a little calmer, the kapos on the other hand, continued with the same ruthlessness.

There was one murder I often think about. It happened a little while before I heard the Russian guns. In one of the alleyways in the camp, a prisoner came across two SS guards. He hadn't done the *Mützen ab* as we were supposed to do in front of the SS, lifting

The Death March, Liberation and Return to France

our cap and standing almost to attention. He had kept his cap on his head. For the guards, he was committing a 'crime of treason', even though he was probably just too exhausted to have noticed they were there. Nevertheless, he had not done the *Mützen ab*. Without even bellowing as they usually did, the SS asked for the prisoner's cap, threw it in the alleyway and told him to go and get it. The poor guy turned around to go towards the cap and the two SS men, calmly, still perhaps talking about the rain or the beautiful weather, or describing their last meal, took out their revolvers and shot him dead. Then they left with as much indifference as when they had strolled into the alleyway a few moments earlier. For them, they hadn't done anything bad, all they had done was kill a Jew. It wasn't a crime to kill a Jew, that was what they were there for. A Jew was not a human being.

In the final days of 1944, I did not see any more acts of barbarity in the camp or in the factory. But I definitely saw many others later on.

I also became aware that the SS were becoming a little disorganised. The look of delight and triumph had gone from their faces. They also looked younger. They had not become guardian angels, far from it, but I felt like something really bad was happening for them.

Did you have any access to information on how the war was going and progress at the front? Or were you completely in the dark?

I was relatively in the dark. It was much later, in October or maybe November, that I heard about the June landings in France.

Don't forget, I didn't speak German, I had very little contact with anyone else and I was still quite young. I didn't know any details of the war or the beginning of the German defeat.

What physical state and mental state were you in by then?

I wasn't as physically tired as I had been before. There were still the interminable roll calls. It was bitterly cold and the hunger still gnawed at me. I was still in squad 55 and without fail I would go to work at the Buna of IG Farben.

Sure, I wasn't in Olympic condition, but psychologically I was feeling better – I could hear the guns. They fed my hope. I thought my liberation was coming and I dreamt of that moment. The sound of the bombings seemed to beat time and count down the small number of days until the Russians would come and open the gates of the camp.

The disorganisation you spoke of just earlier, did that mean life for the prisoners got any better?

Not at all! We still did the same work, we got up at the same time, what we ate was the same. I just had the impression, totally subjective, that there was a kind of relative disarray. It was just a subtle feeling that I can't put my finger on.

Do you think the evacuation of Auschwitz was a spur-of-the-moment thing or it was planned in the days before it took place?

I have no idea. I cannot answer that question. But the Nazis were so convinced of their ultimate victory it seems unlikely they had prepared for our evacuation long in advance.

Do you remember the date of the evacuation?

I think it was 17 January 1945. I think Primo Levi gives that date, but for a long time I had thought it was the 18th. It all happened so very suddenly. Without warning we were all gathered together in the main yard.

The Death March, Liberation and Return to France

I think it was at the end of the day, but I cannot be sure. That whole time was just so bizarre. I was like an automaton. Someone told me to get up, so I got up. We had to assemble in the yard for roll call, so I went. Someone gave me my ration of soup, so I held out my bowl. We had to dig trenches, so I held up my pickaxe and I did it. That day, being the automaton I was, I lost any point of reference, especially any sense of time.

With the SS and the kapos shouting and beating us, we were gathered in the yard in columns of five, and they made us leave the camp just as if we were walking to the factory. But this time there was no music. For the first time there was no music. Also for the first time there were no vicious *Arbeitälteste*.

I vividly remember the departure and the moment we went through those gates for the last time, surrounded by SS, kapos and dogs. When we left we were all in line, then very quickly the long rows of prisoners broke up. We were bumping into each other and the wooden soles of our clogs dragged along the ground, making a kind of continuous rumble.

Did you know that some people (like Primo Levi, for example) remained at the camp?

Not at all. I only found out later, when I read his book.

So how did you feel then? Did leaving the camp restore your hope, or did it concern you?

It didn't really affect me one way or another. I was neither more concerned or more reassured. I trudged along putting one foot in front of the other, like a machine.

However, what did surprise me was the number of SS guards. There seemed to be a lot more of them compared to when we used to walk to the factory. The whole garrison was there in its entirety.

There were also a lot of dogs, usually they didn't have any dogs when we left the camp for the factory. The other surprise was that we were not going to the factory, we were going somewhere else.

Was I anxious? I can't tell you. For some inexplicable reason, the idea that they were leading us to the gas chambers never entered my head. When I had first arrived in the camp I didn't know what awaited me. That day, I was leaving, and I didn't know where we were going. Reliving all those days with the benefit of hindsight over several decades, I realise that I was living like a disembodied puppet, with no reactions. The only flame that still burned within me, even if it was very weak by then, was my imagination.

Was there any change in the behaviour of the SS who were in charge of you? Any worry or agitation? Or did they seem in control of the situation?

What I noticed was the extreme brutality. They were more nervous and ruthless. We were nothing in their eyes. We had to march and they were allowed to do anything to us to make that happen.

Some people couldn't walk any further and they fell down as we trudged along the roads filled with mud and snow. When they fell they were simply killed with a single gunshot and left by the side of the road. Corpses in their striped clothes lined the road. I have never seen so many men die at one time. I have never seen such unbridled brutality.

As we walked along, the gunshots finishing off the living dead broke through the drone of our clogs dragging along the ground. In the camp we had been of some use to them. Our work in the factory was contributing to the Nazi war effort, even if it was only relatively minor. We were, indeed, strong if malnourished slaves, and the SS had earned money renting out our services to IG Farben. On this muddy road and on the dirt tracks, we were of no use to anyone. We just had to keep walking. Keep walking or die.

The Death March, Liberation and Return to France

This terrible Death March went on for several weeks, I believe. What do you still remember of it?

Oh! I remember many things. For me, the Death March lasted a long time as I was not liberated until the beginning of May. From 18 January to the beginning of May, that was almost four months.

It was a very long four months of unimaginable torment. It is no accident that historians have attached the word 'death' to this march. It was ever-present. Death was just lying in wait for its next victim, and it was like I was leaning on the grim reaper's scythe to keep walking.

But we didn't just walk, and walk some more, sometimes we were crammed into trains, railway cargo wagons, where at least I could sleep.

Some really horrendous things happened in those four months. How can you kill people just because they can no longer walk? How can you just leave them by the side of the road? Corpses were littered along the road, marking our route, so the historians were able to follow the great migrations of prisoners.

Long columns of prisoners joined us as we passed by other camps. We also left some members of our group in various camps as we continued on. Everything was a mess, the well-organised Nazi system had gone. That infamous system which in Wannsee, in January 1942, developed the structure for the Final Solution – to kill an ever-increasing number of Jews as quickly and as economically as possible. They had estimated twelve million Jews would be eliminated from Europe once the war was won!

The long columns of prisoners dressed in their convict clothes were fleeing the Allied advance coming from all directions. The aim was to get us far away from the front. The SS pushed us on like a herd of animals but it seemed they were not getting any instructions from their central command. Very few ended up in Prague as I did.

Most columns headed for camps such as Bergen-Belsen or Buchenwald where they were then liberated by the Americans. Historians don't seem to be aware of the column I was in – it is not in the DVD produced by The Foundation for the Memory of the Deportations which retraces different routes taken by the Death Marches.

I remember exactly the beginning of the march when we left Buna-Monowitz. According to some historians we would have travelled sixty to eighty kilometres without stopping. It's possible, but it seems unbelievable. But then everything was unbelievable. What I do remember, like it was yesterday, is that I slept while I was walking! It's incredible but that's what happened. How can you sleep while you walk? I later became a doctor, I studied physiology and I still wonder how it was possible.

There were thousands of us when we left Monowitz, maybe fourteen or fifteen thousand. There were even more of us when we were joined, as I told you, by columns from other camps as well. It was a bit like the car trip back into Paris on a Sunday evening. The cars move forward and then stop, then start moving again. So it is like a kind of concertina. It was the same with the columns of prisoners on the march. When I was in the narrowest part of the concertina, when we were squashed up against each other, pushed by those following behind, I was almost carried along by those around me. I was in such a state of exhaustion that I would lose consciousness, just for a split second. My head would fall on the shoulder of the person in front of me, and then I would snap out of it. I lost consciousness a few times but it enabled me to rest a little.

Are you familiar with the bunch of keys test? You hold a bunch of keys in your hand. Sit in a really comfortable chair, you nod off for a split second, your hand drops the keys to the floor and you wake up. The brief time between consciousness, and the uncon-

The Death March, Liberation and Return to France

sciousness of sleep, that time when you fall asleep still gives you some rest. I went through many phases of ephemeral sleep and all those phases, joined together, enabled me to keep going and keep walking.

I can still hear the sound of the dogs and the bellowing of the SS. I can still hear the sound of the gunshots murdering anyone who could walk no longer, or those who fell to the ground from exhaustion. I can also hear the sound of our clogs. Because we didn't have the strength to lift them, they dragged along the road and made a continuous, thudding sound. When I talk about this time I can still see it all so clearly.

What did you have to eat on the march?

I left Buna-Monowitz with nothing. Some say they left with a piece of bread. I don't know, but me, I had nothing.

In a slightly oversimplified way, when I talk to students I tell them that I had practically nothing to eat in the four months of the Death March. We stopped in a dozen or so camps on the way. At Flossenbürg, at Leitmeritz, those are two names I remember. The other names are buried deep in my memory and I have no wish to retrieve them now. We only stayed overnight in those camps, we were given a litre of soup and then we left again. You cannot say that a few litres of soup in four months nourishes a man. Especially soup for prisoners which was soup in name only!

When the SS got tired (they were also walking, like us) they made the whole column stop, the entire column, and wait in the fields along the roadway. Squatting down in the field, I would collect some snow which I let melt in my mouth, hoping to satisfy my thirst. I also ate grass which I pulled out in clumps!

In these new circumstances did you get close to any other prisoners? Did you talk to anyone else or share any time with them?

I was in my bubble more than ever. It was actually fortunate because how can you live through a march like that without going completely mad? My bubble isolated me from the reality. I remember that time clearly.

At one time on the march, a few solders of the Wehrmacht came to reinforce the guards on our convoy. Taking it in turns, a dozen or so prisoners had to push and pull the carts in which the SS had put their gear. It was very hard work as the road was quite steep, muddy, rutted and full of potholes. Going up was really hard, but so was going down because you had to hold the cart back. The guards had devised a rotation of prisoners at the head of the column to do this backbreaking work. Then it was my turn. I had to pull the cart at the front on the left.

Despite my exhaustion I pulled as hard as I could, but then I slipped in the mud and fell, halting the convoy. An SS guard, shouting insults, pulled out his revolver to kill me, like he had done countless times with others. But a soldier of the Wehrmacht who was standing nearby stopped him.

The SS guard put his gun back in its holster. I imagine he must have been a lower rank than the Wehrmacht soldier. That soldier, the German that he was, saved my life. He then sent me right to the back of the column, with the obvious intention of saving me, and to prevent me from having to pull the cart again.

I often recount this story and tell the students they should not confuse the SS (Nazi activists who enlisted as volunteers) with the Germans of the Wehrmacht. They were human beings like anyone else who is conscripted, like soldiers the world over. There were German SS, but not all Germans were SS. Even if, as some historians have stated, the Wehrmacht often assisted the SS in some of

The Death March, Liberation and Return to France

their killing operations.

In one of the camps where we stopped overnight, the prisoners recognised a *Lagerälteste* from Buna-Monowitz. They grabbed him. He was just like any of us, but now he had lost the protection of his masters, the SS, for whom he had been a devoted servant, doing all their dirty work. He no longer carried himself with the same brilliance or contempt, nor the rage with which he used to beat the prisoners. That day, he was terrified of the prisoners encircling him, coming closer and closer. He was shaking with terror, just like all those who'd had the misfortune to find themselves at the mercy of his murderous hands. He was stoned to death by about a dozen former inmates of Monowitz. I can still hear them shouting as they took justice into their own hands.

You talked about some kind of transport by train. The prisoners were loaded onto trains with no cover for shelter, I think it was.

Not always. I remember on one occasion, we were bundled into some covered carriages, cattle wagons. But mostly we were in cargo wagons with no cover, so we had no protection at all from the snow and the cold.

Did you meet or have any contact with civilians during the march? Do you remember going through any villages where people were still living?

When we went through any villages I got the impression that people were hiding inside, behind their windows. They either didn't want to see, or they didn't want to be seen by the SS, everyone was terrified of the SS. We were not in Germany, we were in Poland and in Czechoslovakia.

There was one thing that happened during the march that really shocked me. Something I discovered later on, after my return to France. The twists and turns and the secrets of memory are quite astonishing. One time, while we were trudging along a muddy track, we saw the entrance to a village called Aüssig, at the end of a long descent. The name stayed in my memory even though the names of all the other villages are lost in the mists of time. The village of Aüssig! But I am jumping a few months ahead in my story. I am now back in Paris and I have been reunited with my older brother who was not deported with us. He told me he had been arrested and taken into the STO[16]. It was hardly pleasant there either, but nothing compared to the Nazi death camps. He told me that one morning, leaving the village where he had been placed, he saw an incredible number of corpses along the road. Dead prisoners dressed in striped clothing. He said he had been in a small village, near Aüssig!

If I had come across my brother in the street in Aüssig, thinking he was free back in France, I could not have walked by and pretended not to know him. I am sure he would not have recognised me, but I could not have been near him without reacting. We both would have been killed by the SS. Why do I remember the name Aüssig when I've forgotten the others, buried in a kind of deep oblivion? It is strange.

What do you think was the purpose of the Death Marches for the Nazis?

Well, I can give you my opinion on that now, but it's just a theory. Most of the SS, fanatics that they were, didn't believe in defeat. I think they still believed in Hitler. They were certainly hoping for their famous secret army to come and bring them victory. They must have figured that after their victory Germany would need rebuilding, and they would need slaves like us to do it. I can see no other logical reason for our leaving the camps.

---

16. *Service du Travail Obligatoire*. A scheme of forced labour which sent French workers to Germany to support the Nazi war effort.

The Death March, Liberation and Return to France

If they had wanted to leave no trace of the camps they could have just burnt them down and killed everyone, which did happen at some camps. They could have just crammed us all into the wooden barracks and incinerated them with their flame throwers. I think they didn't because they still believed in a victory for Nazism. Hadn't Hitler told them that Nazism would rule the world for a thousand years? So, because they still believed the war would end well for them, they needed manpower, forced labour to rebuild Germany, and we would be it.

The moment they lost this belief, they went crazy and were completely unleashed. I remember one especially terrible night. We had been crammed into cattle cars. It was dark and the train had stopped in the middle of the countryside, next to a field or a vacant piece of land, I'm not sure what it was exactly. The SS came along, staggering around and shouting their heads off. They were drunk. They were quite young. I imagine that the adults who had been sent to the front had been replaced by these adolescents who were barely out of the Hitler Youth.

Shouting and laughing at the same time, they chose the wagon I was in and ordered us to get out. There must have been at least sixty of us prisoners in the wagon. While punching us, they made us form rows of five and then they made us do ... gymnastics! I shudder when I think of that night, it was Dantesque. There I was in the dark, doing push-ups, and more push-ups, it was never-ending. Anyone who didn't do the push-ups, or didn't do them well enough, or didn't stretch out their arms enough ... were murdered. I can still see the trace of the bullets leaving tracks of light in the night. Any poor guy they hit was struck like he'd had an electric shock and then he was still. His suffering abruptly ended. The SS guards killed about fifteen of my fellow prisoners. They were completely unhinged. Then we were forced to dig a trench to throw the dead bodies in.

One of the other young prisoners who was also digging the trench forgot to lift his cap and do the *Mützen ab* as he walked in front of guards. They made him stand on the edge of the trench, facing them, so he could see what was about to happen. A few of the SS raised their rifles and fired. The poor guy saw his own death right before his eyes. I will never forget it.

How did I manage to do all those push-ups when I was so exhausted and sick? How did I manage to emerge from that horrific scene without being killed? How was I not paralysed with fear? I had no fear, I was anaesthetised. All these questions will remain forever unanswered.

Those months of wandering led you to Prague where you were liberated. Can you tell us about your liberation?

Yes, but before that, I want to tell you about another thing which, after all this horror, preserved my faith in humanity and in life.

We were in open wagons, you know, the kind of wagons used to transport raw materials, such as sand or rocks. There were still little pieces of coal on the floor of our wagon. It was terrible. We had nothing to eat or drink, we only ate the snow that was falling on us or that we collected from the edge of the wagon. Many prisoners died on that train. To make more room we flung the dead out onto the rocks along the track, with relative indifference – we were so accustomed to death! Other times they were left where they dropped and we sat on top of them. I cannot say for certain that I never sat on a dead person, maybe even someone who wasn't quite dead! That also stays with me. I cannot escape the sadness that overwhelms me when I think of the dead to whom I could show no respect.

Some time before we arrived in Prague the train stopped in a station. Just imagine, these skeletal beings, the living dead dressed like convicts who could barely stand up. Our eyes were the only sign we were still alive.

I clearly remember there were some women in the station. They looked at us with astonishment. All these ghosts, still moving. They had surely never seen a train emerging from hell. Then the train left again.

I think the grapevine was working well, because a few hundred metres further on, I saw an extraordinarily powerful scene. I remember it like it was yesterday. I was in one of the wagons at the front of this very long train. We passed under three footbridges which crossed over the railway tracks. The footbridges were a few hundred metres apart, and they were crowded with people. When the train went under the first footbridge, all the people gathered on the bridge threw bread down to us. In the wagon we were practically fighting each other to get a piece of bread, we were so hungry. I didn't manage to get any, I was too weak and too sick. I must have already contracted typhus. I can still see myself, flailing around like some crazy demon, trying to catch a crust of bread, and missing every time.

I thought they were amazing, those people on the footbridges. No doubt they didn't have much to eat themselves. But they gave the little they had to people who were hungrier than them.

The train continued on. We were coming towards another two footbridges, also crowded with people. The SS realised that the villagers were throwing bread to the starving prisoners. They were furious. They took their weapons and fired up towards the bridge. I saw people fall, injured or maybe even killed. But they continued throwing the bread and the SS continued to fire on them. It was amazing to see the courage with which the people on the bridges persisted with their moral duty as human beings.

That single episode – perhaps a little exaggerated when I retell it now – reconciled me with human nature, if at times I had despaired. I am neither Catholic nor a believer, but having been imbued with Judeo-Christian culture, I felt like the bread from the footbridges was actually coming from heaven, and that the earth was a tomb.

Another strange thing happened. Fate is a fascinating thing, if you believe in it. When I was in the wagon, vainly trying to catch a bit of food, I was so tired that I slipped and found myself at the feet of the others fighting for a piece of bread. Clogs were bashing on my head, bruising my body, and I put up my arms to protect myself. I then saw someone else near me, who was also being crushed by the others above us trying to catch the bread. Then all of a sudden, the people crushing us moved apart and I could stand up in the open air.

Let me play a little with time here and jump ahead a few years. Several years ago I had a little country house near Nogent-sur-Seine, in a pretty village with the romantic name of Courceroy. A friend of mine was on her way home from some thermal baths and she dropped in to see us. She introduced us to her boyfriend. It was hot, we were both in short-sleeved shirts and to my great surprise I saw a number tattooed on his left arm, just like the one on my arm. His number was in the 175000s and mine was in the 167000s. Of course we started to talk about the camps and the Death March. Then an incredible thing happened. We both told exactly the same story that I just told you. There's no doubt that we had been in the same wagon, as he remembered this episode and he also told me about having pulled up a couple of people who'd fallen down in the struggle.

You continued on to Prague on the train. Did you know it was Prague?

Not at all. By then I was terribly sick.

The Death March, Liberation and Return to France

We had stopped in another station, but all the stations looked the same. On the platform, in all languages, the SS were ordering the sick to get out of the wagons. For the first time, I had given up and I had decided to die. I was totally spent, with fever and typhus. I could fight it no longer. I had decided to end it and go towards my death, because to hand oneself to the SS meant certain death. I asked the others with me in the wagon to help me get out. They practically threw me onto the ground, onto the platform, where I landed on a stack of railway sleepers. It was pure chance that I didn't break anything. The edge of railway sleepers is a very hard landing place when you have no muscle left. There must have been about a hundred of us who got out of the wagon. Then the train left again. Once it was far in the distance the SS took off their uniforms – they were not SS, they were members of the Czech Resistance and we were in Prague!

What an amazing story!

Yes, it's incredible. It's like something out of a novel. It's so incredible that I sometimes wonder if it actually happened. It's seems so impossible that I feel like I am making it up. But then I reread the account that I did for my children (some pretty average writing). I wrote it a long time ago, just a few years after my return to France when everything was fresh in my mind, more so than today.

I can just imagine your surprise and joy at seeing those members of the Resistance.

Actually, no. You know, being freed from such a nightmare is not like just opening a door and walking from one room into another. You don't just get straight out of your convict costume. It was not at all like that, at least not for me.

To be free from the camps and the fear of the SS is not like just getting out of prison, for example. Where you find yourself back on the street, free and without chains. I was in such a state of psychological misery that I didn't have the strength to rejoice. I couldn't believe it. I had got out of the wagon thinking I would face death. Instead, liberty and life embraced me. No, it was not as simple as that. Sure I was physically free, but even so, I was not free. One moment, however, I felt a kind of bliss when the nurses brought stretchers and laid me out on one. I became a human being again because they were caring for me, putting me on a stretcher. I was no longer the *Untermensch* who had not known a bed for four months. I was on a stretcher and I had become a human being again.

I had certainly entered another state, but it was not yet freedom. It was only liberation of my body. Real freedom is a lot more than that. The feeling of being free, really free, came many years later. It took many long years before I could feel truly free.

The Wehrmacht were still in Prague at that time, as it was one of the last pockets of German resistance. I think most of those German soldiers were decent guys, they saw everything, but they just let it happen. It wasn't their problem.

I was lying on that stretcher and suddenly a lot of women arrived in the station. I actually didn't know yet that we were in Prague. The women came, and in tears they covered our stretchers with whatever they had found at home: sweets, chocolates and little cakes. I didn't have the strength to even lift my arm to take what I had dreamt of for so long. I couldn't revel in the moment I had so longed for.

Then the nurses put us in ambulances and some of us, like me, found themselves in the Boulowka Hospital, which still exists today. As soon as I got there, in order to wash and disinfect me, a nurse took everything off, including everything else that was on the stretcher. I then felt a real wrench. I was already enjoying the idea of devouring all those delicacies, and she was taking everything.

I was so sad and disappointed by that reception and I cursed her, only in my head of course as she didn't speak French and I didn't understand Czech. "Oh, that bitch, she's taken everything from me." I said to myself.

Over time I have wanted to ask forgiveness from that nurse for having thought ill of her. But at the time I didn't know the pathology of malnutrition. She had confiscated everything, not to keep it for herself, but to prevent me from dying. If I had been allowed to eat everything on that stretcher I would probably have died. That's why she did it. I had to learn to eat again and to get my body used to metabolising normal food again.

She had to cut off my shoes with scissors as my feet were so swollen by deficiency oedema. When I was weighed at the hospital the scales said 35 kilos, and I was 1.77metres tall!

How long did you stay in Prague and what were the conditions like while you were there?

I can't remember exactly how long I stayed in hospital. One time while I was there, the hospital was evacuated and I found myself in a school that had been turned into a hospital, with beds in the classrooms.

I remember two incidents while I was in the school. One day, a former inmate of the camps arrived. He had a beard which was unusual for an inmate. He arrived with a whole entourage, as though he was a politician or someone important. I remember his name, Curda Lipowski. He spoke wonderful French. In the first few years after I returned to France we wrote to each other several times. Then, after a change in the political regime he stopped replying to my letters. Maybe he didn't please the new masters of Czechoslovakia. He was the one who gave me a little money when I was first able to venture out onto the streets of Prague with Vera, my nurse. I still have a photo of him somewhere, which he sent me in one of his letters.

As for the second incident, it could have ended badly. One day, a German soldier of the Wehrmacht came in and looked at all the patients, one after the other. He stopped and looked at me for a long time. I was the only one with a shaved head so I was obviously a former prisoner. Then he just went on and continued his inspection. I sometimes wonder about it. What would the doctors and nursing staff have done if he'd tried to do something to me. I like to think that they would not have stood by and that they would have protected me.

I was quite friendly with the nurse who was looking after me, Sister Vera, even though she didn't speak French. One day I worked out that she wanted to show me her city. They gave me some civilian clothes and the two of us went out. We came upon a square where some German soldiers were being held prisoner, watched over by a guard. The war was over, so it was after 8 May.

Vera and I moved forward to join the other people who were standing around watching them. When the guard saw me he took off his belt to beat the poor guys, who were bare-chested. Maybe he felt that what he was about to do would honour the dead and avenge the suffering in the Nazi camps. The suffering which he thought I represented. He looked at me and he seemed to be saying "You see, my boy, I am getting even for you. They are the ones who must suffer now."

I could not watch such brutality. I had the sad feeling that it was starting all over again. The vile beast had been vanquished but the brutality went on, even if it was now different guards and different prisoners. I was so young. I was just an eighteen-year-old kid whose adolescence had been shattered. With my liberation I thought the world would finally change, that evil and brutality would disappear. It was a rude shock to see that nothing had changed.

The whip, the weapon of violence, was in different hands, but it was there still.

I got out of there as quickly as my poor weak legs could carry me. Vera was shocked and must have wondered for a long time why this young Frenchman had fled like that. The expression, 'Everyone gets their turn', makes me sick to the stomach and I reject it vehemently. Later on, when I was in Paris, I thought about it again and analysed why I had run away from that scene so fast. I had refused to watch what I fundamentally deplored. Brutality had become absolutely and profoundly unacceptable to me.

Vera also took me to an information office set up for former prisoners. I wanted to know what had happened to the people who had been with me on the train. I was told most of them had died on the train or they had been shot. I didn't know any of them; I wasn't friends with any of them (at that time friendship was something I didn't know). But I was devastated. Those martyrs who had gone through all that terror, had survived the horror of the 'gymnastics session'... they had survived the unspeakable, all for nothing. To finish up along the tracks or in a common grave, just when they were on their way to freedom. I would surely have finished up like that if I had not, for the first time, decided to die!

After those weeks in Prague you came back to France. How was the trip back?

At the beginning of July, I came back on a stretcher in an air ambulance of the French forces. We left from an airport near Prague, maybe Pielsen, but I can't remember.

I was in a wide-bodied plane with stretchers stacked up, suspended with straps from the fuselage to the floor. There were two or three stretchers, one above the other. Accompanying us was a nurse of the AFAT – as they called the female members of the French armed forces. The nurse was the first French woman I had seen for such a long time, so I asked her for news from France – the France I had so idealised while I was at Auschwitz-Monowitz. It blew my mind, as young people say these days, to find out that France still had ration tickets. I thought it impossible, one year after the Liberation of Paris! For me, liberation meant prosperity after the long months of deprivation.

What do you remember of your return to France and the reception you received?

My reception in Paris? I have no doubt what I am going to tell you will shock some people.

In Prague I had experienced moments of great warmth from Czech people. Their displays of pure, sincere and spontaneous joy at seeing survivors from the death camps. People I'd never seen before came with us to the airport. They showed us such comforting human warmth. I think they were even sorry to see us go.

A few hours later we arrived in Bourget and the plane stopped in a large field (there wasn't an airport for civil aviation there yet). As with many wide-bodied aircraft, the plane opened at the back. The nurses brought out our stretchers, and there, in the field, there was nobody. Nobody!

I was really disappointed. I had thought someone would have been waiting with great expectation to give us a warm welcome. I was so happy to see France again! I had this idealised view of France which I had so often dreamed of. But instead, what I found was an incredible emptiness.

The Death March, Liberation and Return to France

Sure, I was very needy at the time, but it was still upsetting, there was nothing! Well, not exactly nothing, there was an RATP bus. Probably the same RATP bus that had taken us to Drancy and the Bobigny railway station. Maybe even with the same driver! Just a plain old bus, that was it – when I was returning to my homeland, from the flames of hell in the concentration camps.

We were all packed into the bus, much less forcefully of course, compared to the last time we had been through Paris. During one stop, near a market, a woman came and put a case of fruit in the bus. Apart from that warm and welcoming gesture, I felt like people just looked without seeing us. They looked through me, as though, for them, I didn't exist.

I had this strange feeling that our presence was an embarrassment for them. A little like we were accusing them. Not because of what they had done, because only a minority of the French were collaborators, but more because of what they had allowed to happen. An ethicist would say, with some justification, that one is always responsible for what one does not prevent from happening. Did the people we came across feel the same way?

Right or wrong, what I found on my return to France was indifference, silence and embarrassment.

After that, we were 'stored' – and I don't use that word loosely – in a movie theatre, at a really big cinema. Maybe the Rex on the Grand Boulevards, I can't be sure. I found myself sitting in one of the cinema seats being interrogated by an agent from military intelligence, the counter-espionage agency! I must have been a really dangerous spy! That was also a terrible experience.

Weren't you driven to the Hotel Lutetia?

Not until later. I got to the Hotel Lutetia after the interrogation.

Do you remember the interrogation?

Oh yes! How could I forget it? It was so upsetting. The agent interrogating me asked my surname, given names, date and place of birth, where I was at the time of my arrest, the camps I had been in and a whole lot of questions about things I was trying to forget.

What especially astounded me was that all these people kept coming into the theatre. They would stare at us and then leave. I was like an animal in a cage. People came to have a look and then they left as fast as they could. A monkey you come to look at, but quickly leave in case you get bitten.

So nobody spoke to you?

Nobody at all. There was a Siberian frostiness. You cannot imagine my disappointment. I had expected so much. What exactly, I don't know. Maybe I had always been in my bubble and my imagination had played tricks on me. Perhaps. But coming back to France was such a disappointing homecoming.

After the interrogation I was given the famous *carte de déporté*[17], covered in stamps, together with 7500 francs (the currency of the time), some tickets for a pair of shoes, a suit and some food. I was then put in a room at the Hotel Lutetia.

How did you feel during those first hours in Paris? It wasn't just indifference, was there also distrust?

Absolutely! The interrogation by the intelligence agency, wasn't that a kind of distrust? I can still feel the hair standing on the back of my neck. The government needed to be assured of our good

---

17. A card for those who returned after having been arrested and deported from France.

The Death March, Liberation and Return to France

faith but wasn't there another way, other than to interrogate us like that?

Nevertheless, did you feel happy at the thought of being back in France?

In Prague I definitely felt happy. I had both the good luck and the misfortune to be sick. The misfortune, because being sick is never fun. But it was my good fortune because I was able to meet some wonderful people while being so well-cared for. Vera the nurse, Mr Curda Lipowsky and so many others who brought light to my darkness. Those weeks in Prague gave me the time to gradually get used to being a free man again.

As for the joy of returning to France, it was somewhat soured. Firstly, I was returning alone and then the welcome we received was far from spectacular.

In an interview, Isidore Rosenbaum, a survivor like you, has talked about his liberation and the complex emotions it aroused in him. When asked about the feelings he experienced on his return, he replied, "We didn't have the strength to be happy." This sums up the emotional state of so many survivors when they returned. He also explains it took a few weeks to realise and understand their freedom. Do you share this feeling?

Yes, that's exactly how it was, and perhaps even more difficult. As soon as I arrived in France I very quickly went into my shell. Probably because I hadn't received the welcome I had hoped for. I didn't experience the human warmth I needed so much, and also because I felt no-one in France was even interested in me.

I did everything I could to hide what had happened to me. That doesn't mean to forget, but more to put aside the terrible time from when I was deported. My concealment was such that it became a silence that lasted forty years. From the moment you put aside a period in your life you can no longer feel joy because you are suppressing that terrible time.

Joy can only exist in comparison to sadness. What I hid was the horror, the abomination that was Auschwitz. How could I rejoice at no longer being in the camp when I didn't consciously want to think about that time?

The joy of coming home, the happiness of being free again, which I should have embraced in all its glory, I never really felt at that time.

Human beings are complicated creatures.

So, they put me in a room at the Lutetia Hotel. I felt good physically, but I was very alone. I stayed there three days, with nothing. There was no news of my family, even though I had given them all the addresses where I thought my brother and sister could be told of my return.

You see, from the perspective of human warmth it wasn't great. Sure there was a nurse who took care of me with a great deal of kindness, but I felt that her 'professionalism' didn't really help me psychologically.

Fortunately, there were many volunteers, Jews and non-Jews, who helped with the return of the survivors. They were downstairs in the lobby of the hotel. The daughter of a friend of my mother's was among the volunteers and had asked one of the organisers if there was a Braun amongst the survivors. The volunteer had told her there was, giving her a first name that didn't match anyone in my family. There was another woman in charge who was standing next to her. When she heard the surname she said there was another Braun, Sam Braun, on the third floor. Once I was found, this girl took me to her mother's house where I was reunited with my sister and my brother.

The Death March, Liberation and Return to France

How was the reunion with your brother and sister?

Extremely emotional. My sister and I burst into tears. It was very difficult.

We cried for our parents and our little sister. My tears were all the more intense as the faint hope of ever seeing them again, buried deep within me and held fast, disappeared on that day. From then on I had to live with the fact they had been murdered. Between her sobbing, my sister made me promise to never cry again. I tried to keep my word. I hardly ever cried in public but I expressed my sadness in the communion of solitude, when I cried uncontrollably. Later on, when I was married, when my wife was asleep, I thought back to all those things and I could not hold back my tears.

Can you remember the weeks after being reunited with your brother and sister?

When I met up with my sister again she could see that I still wasn't well. I had a cough and I was so tired. She made me stay at the Bichat Hospital under the care of Professor Guy Laroche. A few years later, at the start of my medical studies, I did my first internship with Professor Guy Laroche, and the ward I was assigned to was the same room where I'd stayed after my return! Coincidence is a curious thing, isn't it?

After a few weeks I left the hospital with a reassuring diagnosis: I didn't have tuberculosis.

While I was in hospital an extraordinary thing happened. In those days we were in a big communal ward, and when a patient was being examined by the doctors, a nurse would put a screen around the patient to provide some privacy. But she would also sometimes forget, which made me smile. The patient in the bed next to me, to my right, was a North African. He had an accent so thick you could cut it with a knife. He loved wine from Bordeaux. In the bed on my left there was an old man who did really well with the ladies. I often played chess with him, each of us sitting on the edge of our beds, the board balanced on our knees. Despite my relative skill at the game, I never managed to win. He was lovely and smiled all the time.

Every day, an old lady with a shaky voice would come and see us during visiting hours. Her name was Gabrielle. I still have her photo in my collection of mementos. She was a street singer, there were still a few of them left at that time. Like something out of Zola, but a cheerful Zola!

This wonderful lady sang in the streets just so she could bring us little gifts, a cake or sweets for the old man and me, some Bordeaux wine for my North African neighbour. She sang in the streets for us and every day she came to spoil us. It was amazing. She was the angel Gabrielle! Afterwards we used to write to each other, then one day, nothing. She lived in the 18th, not far from the Bichat Hospital. She was indeed the incarnation of goodness!

Did you meet up with any of your friends from the time before you were deported?

Yes indeed, in Clermont-Ferrand. When I left the hospital, my brother, who had taken over my father's shop, arranged for me to board in a hotel close to Clermont-Ferrand so I could breathe some fresh air and recuperate. It was in Ceyrat, a lovely little village you reached by tram. The hotel had a big terrace where I sat daydreaming for many long hours. My brother would bring me ladyfinger biscuits. He had asked a bakery in Clermont to make them for me especially. They were the only thing I really enjoyed eating.

The first day I got back to Clermont-Ferrand, before going to recuperate in the village, some friends of my brother's invited me to a restaurant. All the tables were occupied, so the owner asked us to wait at the bar. At the time I weighed about fifty kilos, I had gained about fifteen kilos since Prague! Our friends bought me an aperitif, a martini or a glass of port. But the drink had hardly passed my lips, I'd only swallowed one sip, when I fell to the floor in a heap, unconscious!

Did you want or need to talk about your experience in the camps at that time?

Not at all! I never told my brother anything at all, even though I lived with him for several years. Never. I didn't want to talk about the camps and my brother respected my silence.

I felt so unsettled that I retreated into myself. Sure, from the outside, I seemed happy, lively and even funny. But deep down I was not at all well. The reception we'd received coming back to France made me feel that even if I could have talked about it, nobody would have believed me, so I kept quiet.

I also felt guilty, guilty for living when my parents and my little sister were dead. Sure, I was obviously not responsible for their deaths but I felt a sense of injustice. Injustice that I was still alive while they were dead. I had a feeling of guilt as many others did. Here I was, alive. My parents were dead. It was very difficult to get past that and reveal I had been deported. For me it meant I had survived a world people didn't come back from, and from which I should never have returned. I was here, so that was cause for suspicion. I was here, I was therefore culpable for being here. Of course, I must add, nobody ever reproached me for having survived. Everything was in my head. Maybe I would have responded differently if I had been shown more empathy – that is of course apart from the love and understanding of my brother and sister.

At that time I also had a lot of difficulty accepting my Jewish origins. It is not easy to feel you belong to a community when you don't respect the rituals and practices of that community, or you don't have anything in common with people who follow those traditions. I was not old enough to understand. I probably thought that culture was inextricably linked to religion and a belief in a God creator.

Now I know, or I think I know, and I no longer suffer from being Jewish. I even openly say I am Jewish. But the difficulty I had in accepting myself as being Jewish caused me a lot of suffering in the beginning. I didn't regret being Jewish. Can you regret what you are? But I thought that I had been really unlucky to have been born into this community! I used to hide the number tattooed on my arm because, for me, it represented being Jewish, even though ten per cent of the inmates at Auschwitz were not Jewish.

I remember, during the summer of 1947 I think it was, the weather was really hot and I always wore long-sleeved clothes so nobody could see my tattooed number. I would never tell anyone I had been deported to Auschwitz because I thought it would reveal I was Jewish. I denied it. It wasn't a feeling of shame but I had seen so many people die because they were Jewish – my mother, my father, my little sister – so to be Jewish was a burden. Yes, that's it, it was more painful and a burden than shameful.

How long did it take until you were free of that feeling?

A long time, a really long time. Several years. Am I free of it even now? I don't know.

I was afflicted by three feelings: guilt, difficulty in accepting myself as a Jew, and difficulty living with the indifference of others. That's a lot for an eighteen-year-old fellow!

The Death March, Liberation and Return to France

You have talked about how difficult it was to express your pain and to talk about what you remembered. You also feared you wouldn't be believed and that people did not always react well to what you told them. Was silence the only consequence of those feelings?

I lived with a great burden and such private heartbreak without showing my feelings to anyone. So for a year I turned to alcohol and I became an alcoholic. I drank from morning till night and I only hung out with other drunks. I would go begging so I could drink because I didn't have any money.

Fortunately I was not a real alcoholic, otherwise I would have been dead. But, despite my revulsion for all drug addictions (and alcohol is a drug), I am sure that period of time was actually beneficial for me. It was a real initiation process, in the precise meaning of the word 'initiation', to die in one life and be reborn in another. Being drunk, with the huge amounts of alcohol I consumed, cleansed me of everything I had been through. Just like ninety percent alcohol cleans a festering wound. I just needed to drink, and I drank anything and everything.

My brother suffered because of my drinking – he felt responsible for me but he never judged me in the slightest. He had the intelligence and sensitivity to understand that it was a process. A necessary process for me to go through to then live a normal life.

During that time I also passed my two high school diplomas (at that time you had to sit for two). I must not have looked too bright sitting before my examiners! After falling and sinking into alcohol like a person drowning, having sunk to the bottom I could come up to the surface and give myself a kick up the backside.

Some American psychiatrists have studied the reactions of concentration camp survivors. They say that in a large number of cases the return to freedom causes a period of depression. It's called Survivor Syndrome.

They explain that when a survivor comes home, after the horrific experience of the camps, there is a period of time marked by feelings of really intense guilt, deep depression, chronic anxiety with nightmares, a tendency to become isolated and withdrawn, problems with aggression, cognitive and emotional problems ... The alcoholic phase you went through seems similar to this grim picture.

Yes, apart from the aggression, because even in the grips of alcohol I was never aggressive, at least not to others. But in every other way it was precisely like that.

Joseph Bialot writes, "Only talking to yourself leads to self-destruction." Do you agree?

Absolutely! Nowadays, whenever there's a disaster, a doctor, emergency services and a psychologist shows up. That's the way it should be. But we didn't have any psychologists. That wasn't the way things were done then.

I was only eighteen. My brother was twenty-two and he didn't have the experience my father would have had. My sister was living in Paris and she'd had no experience of being a mother. I had no psychological support, at least not from a professional with the necessary objectivity.

The depressive phase, which led to my drinking, also manifested itself in an inability to talk about what had happened.

Yes, talking can be liberating. If I had been capable of talking about my life and everything I had gone through in the death camp – my childhood ripped away from me when my parents were taken, all the people I saw suffer and die, the barbarity of the SS, the eyes of the dead. All those things were my constant companion. They never left me. But if I had been able to talk about them I would not have needed to drown myself in alcohol. On the other hand, it was alcohol that set me free. I needed to descend into depression to be able to climb back out of it.

On your return to France, in spite of your silence, were you preoccupied with memories of the camp? Or did you manage to block out the painful memories? Did you have nightmares, for example?

Yes, of course, there was one recurrent nightmare. But funnily enough, since I started giving talks to school students I hardly ever have that nightmare anymore.

In the nightmare I am on a high plain. I am running and running, breathlessly running to get away from what is pursuing me. I can hear the sound of boots on the ground behind me. A terrifying sound of boots, the sound of soldiers' boots marching in goose step. I am running to get away as they pursue me. Suddenly, I come to an enormous chasm, like the Grand Canyon of the Colorado. I can go no further. I am blocked by the boots that have followed my trail. I cannot move forward, I am trapped ... I would be so terrified I would wake up in a sweat.

When I was a doctor, I used to have another nightmare related to the time when I was drinking. In the nightmare a 'good friend' comes and says, "You are a doctor, but you never passed your high school exams. You will have to start all over again!" I had that nightmare because I couldn't remember the time when I was doing my high school certificates, because that was when I was drinking so heavily.

But it's strange, in my dreams there are never any images of the brutality in the camps.

You have said that talking is liberating. To put it very simply, one could say that on returning from the camps there were two main types of responses. Writers have basically outlined these in their own way.

People like Primo Levi and Robert Antelme, for example, talked very soon about the need, the necessity, indeed the urgency, to write about their experience to liberate their memories and to tell their story. Then there are men like Jorge Semprun, who describe the need for a long-lasting silence. A silence which later allows them to talk about their experience with the distance of time, sometimes years. In your case, was silence necessary for you?

Absolutely, and for me the silence lasted forty years.

Did silence help you to forget or is it a fragile repression of memories?

To forget, no. It was more a bypassing, to set it aside. Yes, you put it to one side, in a corner of your memory so you can move on to other things and live like a normal person. Silence was important to me because I wanted to get over the camp, to live without being constantly haunted by those images.

In my opinion it is no surprise that some people killed themselves, for example, Primo Levi, who I love and really admire. Many people who talked about their experiences as soon as they came back, they killed themselves, in one way or another. Be it violently, hurting themselves and ending their lives, or more insidiously, talking only about the camps. Bruno Bettelheim, for example, he always said that survivors behaved like autistic people. After being liberated he fled to the United States and created the first clinic in the world for autistic people. That was certainly not by chance. He killed himself a few years later.

Me, I just wanted to get over the camp, to stop being a victim. I couldn't live with death forever. Maybe Primo Levi thought the writing would free him. But I don't think it would have freed me. I believe to really free yourself from this kind of experience you need to keep quiet. Especially to avoid rumination and incessantly looking back at the dark memories.

The Death March, Liberation and Return to France

In The First Man, *Albert Camus has this rigid formula, "When the soul has profoundly suffered it has a great appetite for sadness." A very unhappy childhood can cause intractable suffering in an adult, as if, in a tragic and vicious cycle, unhappiness breeds unhappiness, and suffering causes more suffering. We know that one never emerges unscathed from childhood suffering. What do you think we should do to escape this cycle? How can we get out of this 'appetite for sadness'?*

I would simply say you must not dwell on these things, so you are able to get over them and become a normal person, to the point of being ordinary.

I am not saying to bury things or to forget what you have gone through, certainly not. Because what you have forgotten still ferments in the depths of your soul, and one day it explodes. Getting over the camp meant not talking about it any more, to live, just like other people. Once again, that's what I did and that's what worked for me.

Do you have to accept a period of inertia and silence to be able to re-evaluate your experiences and suffering to achieve greater peace of mind?

Yes, in some way, silence about traumatic experiences which are hard to relive in your mind can eventually unlock your voice and liberate you.

However, I think there are two crucial conditions for doing this. The first is to not think of yourself as a 'victim' in one's past life. To not think of oneself as a victim is really hard, and many have failed to take this difficult step. I know of one survivor who reacted by hating his daughter. He used to say to her, "I was in the camps, you cannot tell me anything." He was using his past life as an absolute reference point, a justification to legitimise his authority and to lay guilt on his daughter. In a way he was taking the moral high ground, using his tragic status as a victim.

I want to strongly emphasise this – we are just ordinary people, if there are things that need to be said, they need to be heard. Having been an inmate of those indescribably terrible Nazi camps gives us no rights. On the contrary, it gives us responsibilities.

I was very lucky because my wife never enveloped me in the role of victim. Whatever happened during my youth I was still a normal person like everyone else, and I want to be accepted by others for what I am and what I have done, not for what I have suffered.

Nor should you make yourself out to be a hero. That's the second danger. A hero is someone who, without hesitation, chooses the most dangerous solution if it's the only way to achieve their goals, for altruistic reasons of course. They choose danger to uphold their beliefs. It's a free choice. As for me, I didn't choose what happened to me, that's why I am no hero. To me this seems to be the only way to mentally get over the camps, to no longer be the *Häftling*, the prisoner. We should not glorify our survival which was only due to luck and particular circumstances.

I am now neither the victim nor the hero of an unfortunate story.

These two conditions are crucial to becoming a normal person with an ordinary life. It is thanks to this outlook that I have, I think, excellent relationships with my children and grandchildren. But to get to such a state of normality I stayed silent about Auschwitz for forty years.

4

To Bear Witness

"Those of us intellectual Jews who escaped death in the nightmare that was Hitler, we have just one duty – to take action so those appalling events never happen again, and also that they are never forgotten or left to fall into the oblivion of the past. We must ensure we maintain our connection with those who died in unspeakable torment. Our thoughts, our work, belong to them. The arbitrary chance by which we happened to escape does not lessen our connection to them, in fact it makes it all the more indisputable. All our experiences must be placed beneath that symbol of terror destined for us, as it was for them. Their death is the truth of our life. We are here to give voice to their despair and to their heartbreak."

Max Horkheimer
Notes critiques pour le temps présent
(Critical Notes for Present Times)

"... besides 'objective' documents, historical memory must consider the irreplaceable experience of the eyewitness – those who have lived through the event. The eyewitness, in fulfilling their duty to remember should, in turn, not neglect the existence of truth which is at the heart of the historian's work. It is on this twofold condition that our collective memory will maintain a connection to the past whilst avoiding mythologising it or allowing it to fall into oblivion."

Jean-Pierre Vernant
Œuvres, Religions, Rationalités, Politique
(Works, Religions, Rationalities, Politics)

I would like to quote a passage written by Aharon Appelfeld (Tsili):

> "Where were you during the war?" asked Tsili.
> "Why this question? With everyone else, of course. Can't you see?" he says, holding out his arm. (The dark blue registration number is tattooed on his skin.) "But I don't want to talk about it. If I start I'll never get over it. I have decided that from now on I will concentrate on living. For me that means to study, well, more exactly to finish my studies."

As Jorge Semprun did, Appelfeld is talking here about the choice to stay silent. During our last interview you spoke of mandatory silence. Nevertheless, do you feel you chose to keep quiet after hearing the first eyewitness accounts?

Clearly my approach was totally different to Semprun's. To keep quiet and to leave what I had experienced at Auschwitz-Monowitz deep inside me, that was not an intellectual choice I carefully thought through. I could, quite simply, not do anything else. I had no choice because I first had to resolve some issues that were very difficult for me. I had to work on myself for several years to get over some things.

I was also aware that if I'd had to talk about it all when I came back, nobody would have believed me. So I just shut myself in my silence and said nothing.

With hindsight I realised that shutting off, my silence about the past, manifested itself in anxiety and nightmares ... which led me to stay silent even longer. Yes, it's strange, silence leads to more silence, like being locked in a vicious cycle.

I may have stayed silent even longer if not for a friend. He was a history teacher in a large high school in Paris and he asked me to come and speak to his final-year students. For a long time I declined. I didn't want to do it. I told myself: "It's not good for you. So keep quiet." I don't talk about it to my wife or my own children, why should I talk about it to other children?

Then one morning, something extraordinary happened. I was shaving in front of the mirror and I suddenly felt like I was looking at a stranger, someone I didn't know. There was someone like me, but shaving with their left hand. An old gentleman, with a wrinkled face and bags under his eyes. Mirrors are not trustworthy, you know, they reflect the image we want to see! I still wanted to be a young man and that's what I used to see in the mirror. But that morning, I realised I was an old guy and I was ashamed of my cowardice. I said to myself: "You're a coward, old boy. The only reason you don't want to talk to the students is because you know it will be painful. Your parents, your little sister and all the others who died there have died for nothing!" I realised I did not have to rationalise the death of my parents and my little sister. That would be unthinkable, their deaths were senseless and could never be excused.

Then it was clear what I had to do: I had to use those terrible events to try to be of some use to young people. To open their eyes to the world and the insanity some people are capable of. That was my one and only purpose. But I didn't want my life in the concentration camp to become some kind of spectacle. So it was on that basis I accepted my friend's invitation to go and talk to his class of final-year students.

However, I didn't go alone. I was so terrified at the idea of being in front of a group of seventeen and eighteen-year-olds. I was in such a state that I asked my friend, Pierre V., to come with me. He had been in the Buchenwald-Dora camp because he was a member of the Resistance. The talk went really well and we chatted with the students for two hours. We took it in turns to speak so the other could have a break in between. After those two hours we looked at each other, happy that it was over, but satisfied we had managed to talk, as we had thought it would be impossible.

Then, unexpectedly, a really special and moving thing happened. Two gorgeous students stood up. One of them was of African origin, the other European. The two girls recited a poem, each taking turns to speak, like two musical instruments playing in a symphony orchestra. The poem was about the yellow star and had been written by one of the French teachers in the room.

When I was in Clermont-Ferrand, I hadn't worn the yellow star, but that star symbolised so many things for me that I burst into tears, sobbing uncontrollably. I just couldn't stop. My friend, despite not being Jewish, perhaps moved by the poem and no doubt by my tears, fell into my arms weeping. It was pathetic! Two sixty-year-old kids wailing in each other's arms!

The yellow star, with the word *Juif*, meaning Jew in French. During the Nazi Occupation Jews were forced to wear the yellow star sewn to their clothing.

Later on, my friend gave my details to some of the other teachers. That's how it snowballed and I started my 'work of remembrance', going to classes to meet with young people. I was doing it at such a rate that, in the school year between 2004 and 2005, I talked to 5700 students (I enjoyed calculating how many there had been!).

So it took a request from a friend to make you talk about your past?

Absolutely! Maybe the request just happened to come at the right time? When I was ready? It's possible, but I can't be sure.

In the years between 1970-1980, given the general mood of the times, do you think there was an evolution in how the Holocaust was regarded? Did this help you change? Could this evolution explain why you then wanted to talk about what happened?

I don't know. Can one really judge how one's psychological state evolves at any given time? It's quite difficult.

Did it help me that intellectuals and the media were talking more about the Holocaust, and perhaps even laying the way for me to tell my story? I don't know, but it's possible.

On the other hand, I do know that my talks were not limited to just my own experience of the Holocaust.

When I talked to the students I went as a victim of genocide, as Paul Ricoeur said, in solidarity with all victims of every genocide in history. I always emphasise this because my mission is to raise awareness. However, I do not merge all acts of barbarity together, because each act is distinct in its own right.

At the beginning, when I started doing these talks, I probably spoke a lot more about what happened in the camp. It's possible. But after a short time I only wanted to 'set the scene', if I can use that term, to describe what happened to my family. This was so the students could reflect and develop their own understanding of what occurred.

You have talked about your tattooed number and that for a long time you had wanted to hide it. Has your feeling about this 'brand' changed over the years? Have you come to accept it?

Yes, I have completely changed. I can pinpoint exactly when it happened. I was a student in my second year of Medicine. I wasn't in a good place. I was always hiding my tattooed number by wearing long sleeves so nobody would see it and ask me about it. I was doing a surgery placement and I was friendly with the intern. One day I told him how I was really embarrassed by the tattoo and that it stopped me leading a normal life. Every time I looked at my arm terrifying images of the camp came back to me.

He suggested he could use a local anaesthetic to remove the tattoo and we organised a time to do it. At that time there were a dozen or so Black Americans enrolled in the Medical faculty in Paris. Remember, in those days in the USA there was a *numerus clausus*, limiting the number of Black students in the state universities. I was friends with some of these Americans, especially one guy called Joe. He was a great guy who had learned to speak perfect French. We used to talk long into the night remaking the world. He was in his second year of Medicine, like me.

Something quite amazing happened. Even though I'd made an appointment with the intern to remove that wretched tattoo and free myself from all my worries, Joe's face came before my eyes like in a dream, and I was ashamed. I thought, "You, you can hide your Jewish origins. You can hide the number that reminds you of being taken to the camps because you were Jewish. He cannot hide that he is Black!"

I had a complete change of heart and I cancelled the appointment. I didn't start telling my story until years later, but at that very moment I began to recognise and accept what I was.

So an acceptance of your Jewish identity and of your past.

At least a start. A start that would lead me to accept my culture.

I want to come back to how it was when you first started telling your story. Did you feel liberated, or more challenged by it? One could imagine that retelling the story plunges someone back into a world of pain, to relive their suffering.

Looking back, now that I have analysed the experience, I see it as the first step in my liberation. At first it was often really difficult to discuss. I have to say, the first few times I would weep in front of the students. Especially when talking about my mother and how she was torn away from me, never to be seen again. I can still see my mother in her pink shawl with my little sister clinging to her, on the truck that took them to the gas chamber. That will remain with me forever as one of the most painful moments of my life.

But it's strange, even though I was so physically bonded to my mother, after coming back from Auschwitz I felt closer to my father. To the point where I imagined myself having long conversations with him, coming up with what I thought would be his responses.

Several years later I realised that talking did indeed liberate me. At first I went through hell, but a little voice in my head kept telling me that talking to young people about what I'd gone through, bringing it all back, talking about my parents, my little sister and all the others I had seen suffer and die – it was good for me and I should keep going.

So do you now feel that telling your story in this way has lifted a weight from your shoulders?

Now I think I can say I am free. After all these years of talking about what happened, some years it was two or three times a week, I have now definitely gotten over the camp, even if it is still part of my memory.

I will tell you three key things that confirm this for me.

I can usually manage to control my emotions which used to sometimes overwhelm me.

The smell of toast is the second thing – I will explain. One day in the camp, I had kept a little piece of bread to eat during the morning. When I got to the worksite it was incredibly cold and the civilian workers had made a fire in a metal barrel. They signalled for me to come closer to the fire to get warm, as they could see the kapo wasn't nearby. For a little treat I took the tiny piece of bread I'd hidden in my clothes and I toasted it on the fire. Then I quickly gulped it down. For the next three days I was as sick as a dog. It felt like my guts were twisted. So for nearly sixty years the smell of toast was unbearable. However, one day a few years ago, without even realising it, I surprised myself by making some toast for my wife. And it was delicious!

And the final thing. Ever since my liberation, I was overwhelmed with grief every 12 November, the date of my arrest. Every year I wanted to go to bed on the 11th and wake up on the 13th. Some time ago I woke up one morning and suddenly realised what day it was – it was 13 November. I had passed over a 12 November without any angst or grief. My memories had found some peace.

Over the time you have told your story and met all these people, has your account changed? I am thinking about an observation made by Jorge Semprun regarding one of his books, The Long Voyage. *Before writing it, he explained, he felt that his memories were dormant. But when he applied himself to delve into his memories to write, and also by the act of writing, his memories were aroused and brought back to life.*

For Jorge Semprun there is a contradictory consequence that results from writing, which he explains like this, "On the one hand, by articulating the memories it enables one to find peace. But on the other hand, it revives the memories." He adds, "Now I have a lot more things to talk about than before I wrote The Long Voyage.*" Did telling your story bring back memories that you had suppressed?*

When I was with the students, the encoding of memory which brings back everything that has been buried, consciously or unconsciously, was revived as Semprun suggests. In a way it also allowed me to somehow more easily access very precise details from the past.

Some especially painful incidents came back to me, most of which I had suppressed. Talking had brought back memories I had repressed so that I could try to lead a normal life. Memories of some incidents were clearer and more intensely real than when I had first started to talk about it all.

Would you say that your testimony has been enriched through the years? Or has it changed?

My testimony has undeniably evolved as a result of my own internal questioning. Why did I need to talk about what had happened? Was it just to tell my story? But for what purpose? Was my story so important?

All these questions have definitely meant I have refined my testimony. I sometimes barely talk about my personal story. What I have experienced has informed my own life, my history, my personality. What I want, and even need, is to pass on what I now know, which is much more than just what happened to me personally. I need to pass on the perspectives my experiences have given me, which is more than just details of what happened to me.

So in this way, what I talk about has evolved. The teachers who have regularly invited me, some of whom have been at my sessions for several years, have very kindly said that every time I speak it is different. It's always different because what I am seeing at the time is evolving and changing. What I talk about is always linked to what is going on at the time, to current events, to life as it is today. The teachers mention the importance of 'living together', which we should be teaching young people. The possibility for a fraternal community of humanity. Even if, for some, such a notion seems unattainable and unlikely.

Having more responsibilities than rights, the work of remembrance for survivors of Nazism and of all acts of barbarity is (even if I am naïvely optimistic) to show that young people and people in general, whatever their culture or origins, can live in harmony and mutual acceptance. My talks have evolved in that direction. Although it is now becoming a little more complicated when you consider the issue of the environment.

The context in which we are living changes from day to day and human beings have returned to madness again. Despite all my hope in humanity – because I do think human beings can progress – my faith is a little challenged these days. Sometimes it even seems that humanity is regressing. Hatred is rising again, using false interpretations of some supposed God as a justification. The madness of the Nazis, conditioned to murder and to be indifferent to the gravity of their acts, has created a precedent. This could happen again, as some still want. But, despite all these indisputable and worrying truths, our duty to the young is to try to convey hope for a better future, a brighter horizon, rather than what is bleak around us.

The sometimes dramatic context you talk about, does it give greater legitimacy to your role as an eyewitness, or does it undermine your account, highlighting its relative nature? After all, one could argue that the world hasn't changed, that genocides still occur, that anti-Semitism still goes on.

In Primo Levi's last writings one can perceive a certain disillusioned weariness when he talks about telling his story to young people. One almost gets the feeling that he is questioning the effectiveness of talking about his experiences. This tragic disillusionment ultimately lead him to silence. There are important questions, it seems to me, in the doubts that he expressed – is telling the story more justified because of the re-emerging threats we see, or is it a tragic futility? Of no use at all?

You raise several questions here.

First of all Primo Levi. He never stopped talking about what happened, from the time he left the camps and returned to Italy. I think the first edition of *If This is a Man* was published in 1947. It actually was not at all successful at that time. Only a few hundred copies, even though it's a remarkable book of universal significance. Primo never ever got over the camp, he was profoundly pessimistic. In reading it I have always felt his despair about humanity. One of his friends, Mario Rigoni Stern, emphasises Primo's pessimism and distrust of people in a book I have just read called *Le Poète secret* (The Secret Poet).

Without wanting to psychoanalyse him, I think his pessimism was mainly due to the fact that Primo did not take the time to leave the camp psychologically. No sooner was he out of the camp than he started writing about the camp, and very early on he was giving talks in schools. This was also at a time when people did not want to hear about what had happened. It was, it seems to me, so much more difficult for him because he was doing this in a country which had been fascist and an ally of Nazi Germany.

In my case, I had taken so much more time to be able to talk about the camp again – forty years. But those forty years allowed me to get over the camp, to put some distance between my life and that experience. So I did not stay in a permanent state of destructive grief.

That said, we must also be aware of our limitations. We are only a fragile grain of sand in this universe. A tiny piece of dust. No matter how good our intentions and our commitment, our influence is quite limited. However, I still retain a measured but strong sense of optimism, even if for some people that's just naïve.

Often students say to me, "There have been genocides before, and also after, the last war, despite the Holocaust. So it has changed nothing!" I answer this way: imagine if a good fairy now appeared in the classroom and brought one person back to life from each generation since Jesus Christ, as a benchmark for example. That might seem to be so far in the past, but there would only be thirty-three generations of sixty-year-olds between us and Jesus Christ. So we need to be patient! Sure, that makes them smile but I believe this idea is important so we don't despair about humanity. We must simply be patient and never remain indifferent to the injustices committed by some people.

Our work with young people is not futile. Especially if they are aware that survivors of the worst hell on earth still have faith in the future of mankind, and despite the barbarity they still have hope for the future. It is this hope that is the foundation of my desire to tell my story.

Just to conclude what you were saying about Primo Levi. I would like to quote an observation that was reflected in many of his interviews. "I know some friends from the camps, men and women, who have completely erased, or have done their best to erase, everything that happened. Some have succeeded. They have, how can I put it, suppressed the memories that were driving them mad. Others can suppress them during the day, but they come back in their dreams. Others keep living inside their memory, that's what I chose." Primo Levi *thus identifies three approaches here: the amnesia approach, the survivor haunted by nightmares, and the eyewitness who talks about what happened. Does the person who talks about what happened continue to 'live inside their memory'?*

I actually see a fourth approach which builds on what Levi describes. It is the survivor who has forgotten nothing, but who, before talking about it, wants to take some time to lessen the pain or to heal in some way. But even with healing there will always be a scar, a scar that never disappears over the years. It remains, forever, a thick scar. Sometimes it itches, other times it bleeds and quite often it even weeps.

As for how much time for silence? I really feel that for most survivors it is imperative to get back to a normal life. How can one live like everyone else if each act of daily life reminds you of painful events in the past? How can you love others if you are permanently reliving the hatred or indifference that our torturers had for us? How can you promote non-violence if you always see the brutality of the kapos?

Is it important for you to become a 'defender of the dead' in your mind? A defender of their memory? For example, Serge Klarsfeld's incredible book, Memorial of the Deportations. *Or the work done by the Shoah Memorial in Paris, with the inscription of each name of those deported to the camps. Is this kind of work legitimate and important in your opinion?*

Of course. I feel such a need for my friends, my parents, my little sister. I started saying to the students – thanks to you, in a way, they live again. Even if I don't always talk specifically about them to the students. Even if I don't tell them that my father's name was Faivel, and my mother was Malka and my sister was Monique.

The Wall of Names at the Shoah Memorial in Paris. The wall is inscribed with the names of 76,000 Jews deported from France and sent to Nazi death camps during World War II.

The fact that I am talking about what happened to them and to countless others, that brings them back to life, just a little.

They are definitely there with me when I talk about Auschwitz, about the gas chambers and the ovens.

Were you especially affected when you saw the names of people you knew on the wall dedicated to those deported in 1943? Or the photograph of your little sister at the Shoah Memorial in Paris?

Of course! I had tears in my eyes and a heavy heart seeing that photo of my little sister at the Shoah Memorial in Paris – a name, a face, a photo of a person make such things real for those who have not experienced them. They also have value as remembrance for those who lived through it. When you put people's names on a wall of remembrance you evoke memories of them. When you see photos everything becomes more real, their life and their death. The Paris Memorial is a little like a cemetery for the Jewish martyrs of France.

A few years ago I went to Warsaw and I visited the site of the ghetto, at least what little is left of it. Bollards along the path are inscribed in Polish, German and English, to describe what happened there. Two houses have been preserved, like mementos, to bear witness for all the ghetto.

Around the corner, in a little laneway, there is a wall similar to the memorial wall at the Shoah Memorial in Paris. There are only given names on that wall, the given names of Polish Jews who were deported. I saw the name Faivel, my father's name. I saw Malka, my mother's name. For me it was as if my father and my mother were inscribed there, even if there were only given names, and neither of them had lived in the Warsaw ghetto!

The Wall of the Righteous on the outside wall of the Shoah Memorial in Paris. The wall is inscribed with the names of more than 3,900 people who saved the lives of Jews in France during the war.

Allée des Justes (Laneway of the Righteous) is the lane next to the Wall of the Righteous. The sign reads: In honour of the Righteous who saved Jews during the Occupation.

I would like to come back to a time in the past. On returning from the camps, writing could sometimes be used to preserve memories, but also as a refuge in the face of the prevailing deafness and enforced silence. For example, as the psychoanalyst Régine Waintrater explains, "Few survivors could talk to their loved ones about what they had experienced and they withdrew into themselves, choosing the blank page as their only confidante."

You have talked of having written an account of your experience for your children and your friends. Can you tell us about what you wrote and what you now feel about that text? Did you feel the need to write your story because you could not talk about it?

Exactly. I had a kind of need to ensure those memories would survive me. I particularly wanted my children to know all about their past. Because my past is their past. It is as much theirs, as I often say they were there with me in Auschwitz. Because, without wishing to of course, I weighed them down with my angst. I thought writing could fill in what was missing because I was not able to talk with them directly.

I wrote that text several years after my return to France.

I gave a copy of it to my wife and one to each of my children and asked them to read it when I am no longer around. I don't think they listened to me!

I didn't open it for about thirty years. When I read it again a few months ago I had tears in my eyes. Some scenes that I hadn't wanted to remember, I had just 'spat them out' into that book. I found some things I had not discussed at all with the students, or to anyone else. That upset me.

I had called this little text *Les larmes d'Auschwitz* (The Tears of Auschwitz). Tears I shed when I read it again. And because barbarity is still rampant in the world, at first I wanted to call it *La fumée sort toujours des hautes cheminées d'Auschwitz* (Smoke is Still Coming from the Tall Chimneys of Auschwitz).

You once shared with me that you were not really happy with what you wrote.

Yes, because I thought it was incomplete. It had only one purpose, to explain to my children what I could not tell them face-to-face. The text only described events, completely obscuring the lessons I learned there. That's how it is deficient as an account and quite badly written because I 'spat it out'.

Have you, like many people who went through the camps, felt that you were unable to capture or relate in words the tragic magnitude and unique horror of it? For example, Aharon Appelfeld, in his autobiographical book, Histoire d'une vie *(Story of a Life), talks about a "feeling of only scratching the surface". Do you feel you only scratch the surface when you try to describe your experiences?*

That's the major problem with the written language. You need an extraordinary talent to get even close, let alone adequately describe some things. It's impossible. You can only scratch the surface, as Appelfeld says, when you are trying to recount what happened. It is so completely out of the normal range of reference, so bizarre, that we just don't have the words. Even a gifted writer like Primo Levi could not adequately describe the stench, the bewildered look in the eyes of the inmates. Their eyes wide with terror, their screams.

That's the inadequacy of the written word compared to speaking. Together with words, speaking uses a whole range of other elements – sound, voice and melody – which combine to give substance and strength to the spoken word. I feel so much more at ease in front of a camera when I can include sound and melody to enhance the words I say. In a way, a written sentence can suppress spontaneity because you read it and then read it again. You correct it, you look for the right word. You often delete the first draft which is the only spontaneous thing in writing. When you are saying something it may not be perfect but it doesn't really matter, the tone of your voice makes up for any imperfection.

I am far more comfortable with the spoken word than I am with writing. For me it seems more authentic, as the melody of a word arouses emotion.

When someone is giving their testimony, should they only describe what happened or should they try to include perspectives they have subsequently developed?

Let's leave it to the historians to take care of writing history. We cannot do it. We will never remember enough. Nor will we have the necessary impartiality to be writers of history. We should also allow ourselves, when necessary, to leave out some details because some things we went through are simply indescribable.

It seems to me to be far more important to point out certain truths. There have been people who killed other people, purely for what they were, without any other justification than that. What did they do with the dead? They used them for raw materials. Human hair to make fabric and to line the boots of soldiers on the Russian front. Gold teeth to make ingots that are probably still today in the vaults of some banks. They were even planning to make soap from the fat produced by the crematorium ovens.

It was genocide because, as well as committing a crime against humanity, they added the desire to persecute individuals and wipe out an entire group of people. This genocide was also distinctive in that it was state-sanctioned genocide. If one places this appalling story at the heart of human barbarity, while of course recognising its uniqueness, the role of eyewitnesses is not limited to just telling the story, as this in itself has no intrinsic value for young people. However, what seems to me to be essential is to demonstrate that this gentleman, who lived through these atrocities, still has faith in the future. He believes in humankind and in its ability to change for the better.

Moving away from a strict retelling of events, does the eyewitness risk going beyond their role and losing credibility?

The eyewitness can move away from a strict retelling of events, like I do with young people, and move into other areas, for example more philosophical areas. When one does this there is undeniably a risk of not being seen as a reliable eyewitness. What is an eyewitness account in the minds of some people, if it is not the most accurate account of events told by those who were actually there?

As soon as one talks about 'the art of living together' for example, one stops being an eyewitness in the strict sense of the word. Because in their refusal to see us live, what the Nazis taught is the opposite of the art of living together.

But what matters to me in giving my talks is that they have a purpose. In fact, what matters to me in the story I bring to young people is relationships between people. That's because the Nazis denied us even the idea of life itself. So I try to teach young people to respect the lives of others. I don't want to be one of those people who says, "You must suffer because I suffered, cry because I cried."

I encourage the opposite in young people. To act to reduce the weight of human suffering. To not give in to the heartlessness that threatens us all. I know I can be accused of being innocent and naïve, but I would rather that than inaction and silence.

In a way, the account of someone who has lived through something enriches history?

History is written using documents and preserved archives. But with the Holocaust a lot of primary sources have been destroyed. While it is still possible to collect them, the testimonies of those who lived through this provide a better understanding of how the camps operated and the inhumanity endured. They allows us to understand the suffering, the dehumanisation, and the systemisation of death and extermination at work in the camps. In my opinion there is no contradiction between history and eyewitness accounts, rather, they are interrelated. History is nourished by people's memories.

It is sometimes said that the 'duty to remember' can be detrimental because it means one remains trapped forever, looking back at a past of the cruellest kind.

I agree with such criticism if people limit themselves to only, what I call, the duty to remember.

By contrast, the work of remembrance is something else. This is more directed towards the future, thus not dwelling on the past when discussing what happened. Rather than concentrating on being a victim, we should teach what we have learned about human beings and their frailties.

How do you distinguish between the duty to remember and the work of remembrance?

I will try to be clearer. The work of remembrance can be summed up like this: I have mourned. I will do all I can so that you, in turn, will not mourn. And you, you will do all you can so that now and in the future, human beings will need not mourn injustice. Whilst the duty to remember seems to be: Look how much I have mourned. Feel in your soul what I have suffered and feel sorrow for my suffering.

The duty to remember is a return to the past, to a collection of memories and past events the survivor has experienced and recounts to others. The work of remembrance is to use the past as a way to reflect on the present and to look to the future. Ricoeur said, "The only value of memory is if it leads to change." That is to say, if it makes us look ahead to the future and if it helps us to improve people's lives. Boris Cyrulnik also declared, "There is no duty to remember, but there is a duty to do something with what one remembers. To have a plan."

We should leave writing the story of the past to the historians. The eyewitness is too involved, too personally affected to be able to write about it dispassionately. They cannot aquire the necessary perspective with regard to what happened. Our task as witnesses is to carry on the work of remembrance which means trying to affect those who listen for the better, even if just a little. Or, at the very least, make them ask themselves some questions.

The perpetrators of the barbarity we suffered were just ordinary people. They were not insane, even if they committed unforgiveable lunacy. They were ordinary beings, like you or me, like all of us. So, in some circumstances we could all become the perpetrator if we are not vigilant. That's what we must explain to young people, so they are vigilant, firstly with themselves. Barbarity is not only the preserve of others.

I also try to ask myself, what is the tipping point that makes a monster out of an ordinary person? We must always look at ourselves to avoid such unforgivable deviations and to look towards the progress we wish for.

Sam Braun

When the concept of a duty to remember emerged it was, I think, to show the importance of never forgetting the Holocaust, at a time when the genocide of the Jews was again being overlooked. People really didn't want to listen to the victims or to look at the existence of such appalling inhumanity – it is so shocking for a supposedly evolved Western civilisation. There was a time when people did not want to hear, a time of guilt and of blame. Then, at the end of the 1970s, the deniers appeared, those who Vidal-Naquet called the 'assassins of memory'. They made a big noise despite their very small numbers. Incidents such as the attack in Rue Copernic[18] in 1980 and the resurgence of the Far Right, as well as the rise in strident anti-Semitism, these explain the urgency felt by survivors like Primo Levi, and the 'duty' to speak up and talk about the Holocaust. I have been quite surprised at how thoughtless some people are when they question the duty to remember. Some say, why dwell on the past and go over these things we already know about? They forget that for coming generations the Holocaust needs to be interrogated more than ever.

All the same, we may also wonder if the rise of anti-Semitism these days means that we have a duty to remember more than ever, along with a duty to history. Young people must study this period in history. They should also listen to, read or watch the accounts of survivors so they can understand these individual and unique human tragedies.

Of course. The duty to remember is necessary to give the survivors back their voice, for them to share their stories and to preserve them for the future. But there are limitations if such stories are confined only to memories. Faced with these memories, one risks being frozen in shock and only dwelling on the incomprehensible tragedies that occurred. The work of remembrance can fill the gap here.

---

18. On 3 October 1980, terrorists bombed the synagogue in Rue Copernic in Paris. Four people were killed in the attack.

This can only be done if the duty to remember has first been attended to. This is because the principles of 'a good life', in the humanistic meaning of the term, are founded on behaviours, opinions and actions that people must uphold, in order to avoid becoming perpetrators of barbarity themselves. These reflections are especially relevant when looking at the genocide of the Jews and of the Romani people, which must not be forgotten.

One can also look at the example of World War I. Those who went through it long talked about it as if it was some kind of adventure, a pinnacle of glory for a soldier.

There was never any real work of remembrance, a more critical view of that time. We had to wait many long years before anyone dared to speak about the horrors of that war, or to hear stories from some soldiers, telling us it was appalling, terrible.

No, World War I was not an adventure, it was horrendous carnage. A merciless nightmare for those poor soldiers, both French and German, who rotted in the mud of the trenches. Imagine if afterwards the soldiers had felt it was their duty to carry out a work of remembrance rather than just limit themselves to telling the story. Maybe the second war would not have been so horrific. Maybe.

Were there any memorable reactions from students when you were giving your talks in high schools?

Oh yes! I will tell you a story. Two years ago I was giving one of my talks in a school in 93.[19] It was a disadvantaged school with a high immigrant population. I was talking in the school library and the space wasn't really suited to the purpose. There were round tables and some students had to sit with their back to me, even though

---

19. 93 refers to the first two postal-code digits of a disadvantaged outer suburb of Paris.

the librarian had arranged it so there were as few students as possible who had to sit like that.

A young North African student arrived, and from what I could tell he was deliberately late. He sat himself at a table and very obviously turned his back to me. The librarian intervened and got him to move. After making his dissatisfaction known, the young man moved himself to sit behind a column. I couldn't see him but he wanted me to know he was hiding from me, almost provoking me and overtly showing his disinterest in everything I was saying.

Then someone asked me about the Israeli-Palestinian conflict and about the children who had been killed during that conflict. I replied sincerely, saying that for me nothing justifies the death of a child, no matter their origins or beliefs, and such a death always breaks my heart. I kept on talking and answering questions, some of which were quite difficult. Gradually, all on his own, without anyone saying anything, I heard the scraping of a chair moving. The young guy had moved forward to look at me. He looked at me without any animosity or anger. He looked at me as a man who, despite having suffered so much in his youth, carried no hatred and could still see sorrow. A man who gives every human being an equal place in the grand scheme of life.

There are also lovely stories such as a comment from a student at a high school in Lille. He got my attention. Then, in a strong accent which was part North African and part Northern French, he tapped one hand with the other, trying hard to come up with the word he was looking for. Then he asked, "Sir, Sir, have you always had your, your, your … barcode?"

It was obviously not said with any kind of malice or provocation. It was so funny I had a good laugh!

When I first heard you talk I was quite amazed at just how captivated the students were while they were listening to you.

Yes, I have often noticed how intently the students listen when I talk about these things. A few days ago I was invited to a town in the country. I had to talk in front of 350 students following on from a production of a beautiful play written by Helene Daché, based on one of the texts of Charlotte Delbo, called *Auschwitz et après*. (Auschwitz and After)

It was amazing. The play was wonderful and I had in front of me 350 adolescents who had just watched a sad and sometimes difficult piece of theatre. It was very moving. There was complete silence. You could have heard a pin drop. I felt a real connection with all those young people.

Have the testimonies of any other survivors been particularly important for you? Have they made it easier for you to talk about your own experiences?

I have read Primo Levi, and I have read Semprun because he's a great writer, and several others as well.

I read Primo Levi because we were in the same camp. I didn't know him but I was curious to see how he would describe it. I have read almost all his books. However, I have seen very few films. I have never seen *Nuit et brouillard* (Night and Fog). I have never seen any documentary films, except *Shoah* by Lanzmann, which I was invited to. What could all these films do for me, except bring more sorrow and suffering?

What about films that are fictional, like Life is Beautiful *by Benigni?*

I have seen that film, but in quite particular circumstances. I was invited by an organisation, Mémoire 200, which was using this film to introduce a discussion on remembrance for students. I saw it with several hundred young people.

I loved it for several reasons. First of all, it is not a film about Auschwitz. The prisoners' clothes were too clean, too well-ironed.

Benigni's son could not possibly have ever been at a table with SS children! The whole film is a fiction and it makes no secret of that. Also, the film is a comedy and treats anti-Semitism with derision. Remember the extraordinary scene in the first part of the film, when the hero plays the role of an inspector at the academy of anti-Semitism and makes fun of all its beliefs.

I liked the second part of the film for other reasons. I saw a little of myself in the young boy (even though he was a lot younger than I had been in the camp). His father often said to him, "Everything you see here is just a game. And if you play it well you will get a thousand points and win a tank." So the little boy started dreaming, just as I had escaped by living in my imagination.

Some people have criticised the things you appreciated about the film, its fantasy and the lack of reality.

No film can be realistic and portray what really happened.

What do you think of the quite emphatic position that disparages any fictionalisation of the Holocaust?

One day, a group of high school students came to see me. They were working on a difficult topic as part of their TPE,[20] "Can fiction, in any form at all, truly describe the reality of the Holocaust?"

We discussed their topic all afternoon. It was quite intense. We concluded by saying that one form of creative expression alone is not enough to be a 'conveyor of memory'. However, perhaps a combination of several forms of creative expression could get close to reality. What would a film be without the dialogue and the

---

20. *Travaux Personnels Encadrés* is a research-based project which is part the curriculum in the second last year of high school in France.

integration of music? Isn't a photograph so much more powerful when one is aware of the story behind it?

But even if fiction cannot portray reality it can allow us to get closer. To imagine. To reflect. It is far from inconsequential.

Jorge Semprun also defends fiction to convey memory – fiction maintains memory. Imagination takes us into unknown places outside ourselves. "It is necessary for writers to capture these memories. If imagination doesn't take over from facts, the reality of memories will burn itself out."

As long as one does not plunge into an overly romanticised world which is far from reality. Semprun sometimes uses his imagination but it is firmly based on reality.

Do you think films that collect the testimonies of eyewitness and survivors, such as Shoah *by Lanzmann, are important?*

Yes, they are extremely important. Especially the very moving testimony of that hairdresser, a former member of the *Sonderkommando*, who is now in Israel.

It also seems to me that Spielberg's work is very important. But it is important in another domain, because the interviews he has recorded with hundreds, indeed thousands, of survivors will be an irreplaceable source of information for researchers. It's essential to have such a repository of information.

As for Lanzmann's film, apart from the quality of the testimonies, it has the virtue of being the first major film that genuinely gave a voice to the eyewitnesses.

Do you think we need to find a way to ensure that these testimonies are always remembered? How can we pass these stories onto the next generation, when the survivors are no longer with us?

I have a very personal opinion on this, which could be questionable.

First of all, I believe that only those who lived through these things can pass on the stories. Only those who saw these things first-hand can adequately describe to anyone what happened.

For me, a person who can keep the memories alive is something else completely. It is a person who is passing on or continuing the work of remembrance, providing a perspective on what is it to be human after Auschwitz. They must impart their faith in humankind and in its ability to change for the better. To pass on the message to not just love others, but to also respect others.

If human relationships are only guided by love, and if respect for the dignity of the other is not paramount, you can use love as a reason to scratch someone's eyes out. In the name of love, I have often seen one person in a couple become a tyrant who controls the other: "I love you, and because I love you I know what is good for you (!)". And, in the name of love, one person can feel obligated to support things they definitely do not want to support. I have sometimes seen people taking almost dictatorial positions where there is love but there is no respect for the dignity and freedom of the other.

Those who pass on memories have a mission – to pass on a desire and a way for us to live together. To respect others no matter the colour of their skin, their religion or their culture.

But first and foremost, this requires a genuine effort to look at yourself. You must do everything to ensure these values are integral to your everyday life. To fight against our weaknesses and faults. Allow me to use an example I've borrowed from a philosopher (whose name I have actually forgotten): "We must live according to our values hoping that someone is watching us." That is not always easy!

The philosopher Jean-Pierre Faye (La Déraison antisémite)[21] *explains that any account of the Nazi era must also talk about the actions of the Righteous, all those people who took action to save Jews during the war, sometimes at their own peril.*

He quotes several examples. In Denmark Jews were protected and relocated to Sweden. Also in France, in Chambon-sur-Lignon, the entire, mainly Protestant, population hid and protected Jewish refugees.

Should we also pass on and examine the stories of what the Righteous did?

Yes, because this is something rooted in the most profound sentiment at the core of an often fallible humanity.

The Righteous should hold an important place in the duty to remember. The stories of what they did must be recorded. Their example should especially inform the work of remembrance to interrogate why they took the decision to risk their lives for others. That's an important topic to investigate.

I have already told you of the courage of the Czechoslovakians who threw bread to us from the footbridges while the SS took aim at them with their machine guns. They were remarkable but they were just doing their duty as human beings, as we hope all people would do.

The work of remembrance strives for the future. We should honour those who realise they are part of the community of humanity and reject the savage nature present in all of us, which manifests as fear and stupidity. To foster hope we must highlight human beings who behave like human beings.

Who were the Righteous, now called 'The Righteous Amongst the Nations'? Human beings who simply behaved like human beings, seeing Jews as equals, as their fellow human beings.

---

21. Translation of title: The Madness of Anti-Semitism.

The Righteous did their duty as human beings, but as a calibre of human being that most have not yet attained, far from it. A human being who has reached the ultimate stage in the evolution of humanity. When I speak to students I always use the Righteous as examples, so they understand why we must not despair about the nature of humanity. Even if the actions of the Righteous were exceptional!

5

Return to Auschwitz, Forgiveness and Humanism

"Forgiveness, if it exists, should and can only apply to the unforgiveable and indefensible – and thus it does the impossible. To forgive the forgivable, the justifiable, the excusable, what one can always forgive, that is not forgiveness."

Jacques Derrida
Le Pardon
(Forgiveness)

"Forgiveness is the only response which is not a reaction. It is an action that works in a novel and unexpected way, independent of the act that provoked it. Consequently, it frees the forgiver from the consequences of the act, as well as the forgiven."

Hannah Arendt
The Human Condition

Sam, I believe you went back to Auschwitz a few years ago?

Yes, it was in 1995, more than ten years ago.

Can you tell us about it? Why did you decide to go back there?

I had wanted to go there for a long time. I had an inexplicable need to return to the place where my parents and my little sister died. But it has only now become clear to me why I had not revealed that need for so long. Nevertheless, I felt the need intensely. I was not able to go back to the actual camp I had been in. That's because the Buna-Monowitz camp, which was constructed to supply slaves to be hired out by the SS to IG Farben, was completely burned down by the Russians. There is nothing left. Only a memorial stone remains, that's all.

I wanted to go back to Auschwitz before I died. I wanted to return to where my family took their last steps. Maybe I would find their footsteps still left in the snow. Every year on 2 November, Christians pay their respects and commemorate all the deaths there. Nothing remains for me in that place, like all the children of Auschwitz victims. There was no burial shroud for my family, there is no grave. All that remains for us is what still lives on in our hearts. But the need to go back there really haunted me, it was so strong.

There was a trip being organised in 1995 and I quickly put myself down to go. My wife wanted to go with me. "There is no way you are going without me." she told me. I felt I had no right to impose such an ordeal on her. But I can honestly say that I was so touched by her instinctive response. Life is a lonely adventure. I was going back to my past, but with my wife beside me I would no longer be alone and I could face it head on. I could calmly deal with this first trip back, because the woman I love would take me by the hand and her presence would bring me great comfort.

Fifty years earlier I had been abruptly thrown into a world of indescribable madness. After the SS had torn my family from me I had suddenly been completely alone. Alone, I had struggled to survive and I made it, even though I had been unprepared to deal with this crazy world.

My wife called my four children and three of them, without a moment's hesitation, decided to come with us. "There is no question of Dad going there without us," replied my youngest son. "As a free man, he will not return alone to the place he was in chains." Only my eldest daughter did not come with us, confessing to me that she was not ready to take that step. I completely understood and I agreed with her decision.

So we went, the five of us.

The visit was really, unbelievably emotional for me. Not just because I was seeing those places again, bringing back the exact, heartbreaking things that had happened. But it was also very emotional because I was going back with my family. I walked under the main gate, under the words "*Arbeit macht frei*", "Work sets you free". Now that I knew what work meant for the SS, I also knew what 'freedom' meant for them. I burst into tears. I leaned into my wife and daughter who enveloped me. The whole time my youngest son had his steady hand on my left shoulder, as if he was protecting me. My oldest son never left me for a second. I think he thought I was going to collapse! It was a really profound experience. I needed to make that journey. It wasn't particularly rational, I needed it without really understanding why. I also hadn't realised just how important it was to have my wife and three of my children by my side in that place.

The whole time, despite the fact I had been silent for too long, and despite the sound of my uncontrollable sobbing, I felt that my family understood. Without any further explanation it was as if a kind of veil was lifted between us. I was relieved. Not because of

Entrance gate to the main camp at Auschwitz carrying the words *Arbeit macht frei* – Work sets you free.

Return to Auschwitz, Forgiveness and Humanism

what I hadn't said before, but because of what I no longer needed to say. That day they could breathe the air of Auschwitz with me, and also with the members of their family whose lives had been stolen by the SS. From then on I had a strange feeling that my role had changed and I was not the father of my children anymore. In a way I felt I was now their child, as they were so protective, so comforting, surrounding me with love. It was as if now that I had nothing more to tell them about Auschwitz, I had nothing more to teach them. What was also amazing was that I felt the same way about my eldest daughter who hadn't even been with us that day!

Like all the pilgrims returning to visit Auschwitz, we entered through the main hall which was like a reception area. There were three glass cases, three large glass cases. One was full of hair, all grey. It had aged on its own. Another case was filled with shoes, and another full of pairs of glasses. At the bottom of one of the glass cases, I can't remember which one, there was a doll. A little ragdoll. I cried so hard. I imagined a little girl going into the gas chamber clinging to her ragdoll, desperately trying to protect her doll from the suffering that was about to befall her! It was so powerful.

Near the glass cases, I can't remember where exactly, there was an urn on the floor, a large urn filled with ashes. The ashes had been collected from the crematorium ovens. Then, my wife took three roses from her bag; she had brought them with her from Paris. She set them into the ashes to honour my parents and my little sister. It was an extraordinary moment and the only time we all wept together – my wife, my children and me. We wept for my family. It was such an incredible moment that we shared, of such intensity and intimacy. As I talk about it now, more than ten years later, I can still feel the profound emotion of that visit to Auschwitz. I think the experience helped us to move forward and perhaps even grow a little.

Do you think this pilgrimage would have been possible a few years before that?

Not for me. Certainly not. The need to confront my past had to first rise up within me. I needed to wait until my soul demanded it. I had to first walk alone in the solitude of my being. That first phase would later lead to my being able, years later, to return to Auschwitz with my wife and my children. It was, as I have explained, a long time, oh yes, a very long time before I could accept that it was indeed time for me to come out of my hiding place in the shadows. Time to uncover what was dormant and to have the strength to confront it without too much suffering.

Going back to visit Auschwitz was extremely gruelling. I wept all afternoon. The whole afternoon I could not hold back. I wept shamelessly, as if the sixteen-year-old boy was being reborn, and through me he was weeping the tears he had not shed when he had been there all alone. I could not stop weeping. Did I even want to stop? Hadn't I been waiting fifty years for these tears? Stifled tears, buried deep in my heart?

When we arrived on the platform at Auschwitz-Birkenau, which wasn't the same platform where my convoy had stopped back in the past, I didn't recognise anything except the symbol of the station which the whole world knows so well. I had not noticed it back in 1943. But I did recognise one thing, there was a smell, indefinable and ever-present in my memory. We visited in the month of March, whilst it had been December when I had first arrived there in 1943. So the weather was not the same but it was still cold. However, the smell was still there. Indescribable. They say that the strongest memory is that of smell. Does death have a specific smell? Because it was still there, on both those two platforms, the one on which I had been deposited in 1943, where I had seen my parents and my little sister for the last time. And on the other, the present-day platform where I stood in 1995. Was it death that connected them? Yes, it was a particularly difficult experience, but it was valuable.

I felt like I had finally arrived at the end of a long journey inside myself. A journey that had gone on for years. I was always searching, afraid of finding myself. From the moment we got back to Paris, that same evening, I felt enormous relief as if the unbearable weight of silence had finally been lifted.

After the trip to Auschwitz I didn't need to tell my children anything else. They understood it all.

Did your children want to find out any more after that trip? Did they talk more to you about the trip or talk about your past?

Not directly. They never asked me any questions. Never. However, sometimes one of my children came along when I was giving a talk. In fact they sometimes all came together. I think I was able to impart some of those memories without using any words. It is not always essential to talk. That day at Auschwitz they understood everything without my having to use words which were too hard to express, and they are now able to carry on the remembrance. They have inherited a legacy that belongs to all humankind; because such acts of barbarism are part of this legacy.

As someone who has gone through Auschwitz, what do you think about what you discovered there on the day of your visit? Were you immediately overtaken by emotion or did you limit yourself to looking at the displays and how the place was presented?

I had mixed emotions. Of course there was intense sorrow, as shown by my weeping. But also, I had a horrible feeling that the past was almost theatrical. Everything that happened seemed like it had been part of a play in the theatre. I felt I had come into the

Sam with his wife and children.

Sam with his daughter, Malka.

Return to Auschwitz, Forgiveness and Humanism

temple filled with spiritualists and merchants, like a kind of market of suffering.

I never forget how important it is to set the scene for people, in order to jolt the human consciousness. I also know it is necessary to explain to the pilgrims to Auschwitz how these events happened in reality. That way they will understand and then be able to pass it on to others, so these things are never forgotten. But for me, who knew it all, it was quite hard to listen to a guide reeling off a script they had learned by heart, in a monotonous and unfeeling voice.

Such places should also be silent places. It is important for the visitors to just hear the silence. Unfortunately, that wasn't the case, which was really hard for me. But I am full of contradictions – I tell you that, and then I go to schools and talk about what happened.

Auschwitz is not a ghost town. The dead are still present; they are all there. And because it is not a ghost town, Auschwitz requires that the pilgrims listen to the silence. A silence inhabited by such suffering.

Did the way the site was presented seem distasteful to you?

No. I believe Auschwitz has been left in the state it was found, as it had previously been barracks for Polish soldiers. That is, apart from the first room we went into, which obviously didn't used to have glass cases and an urn filled with ashes (which I told you about).

Before we entered the camp we walked along the rows of barbed wire which used to be electrified. There was a very large, black crucifix. That upset me terribly. It was as if the site had been appropriated. I would have been just as upset if I had seen a large Star of David. My parents, and a great many other Jews, were murdered there even though they were not religious. I am not against religious expression, each to his own, to believe or to not believe. But such things should not be proclaimed in that place. It was not just because of their religion, that is to say their spiritual convictions, that the Jews were murdered. It was only because they were born Jewish! Auschwitz should be a place of silence, where one should only hear the sound of the stones and the wind whispering of the misery endured there. It should also be a place where religion is irrelevant. There had been people in Auschwitz who had converted to other religions but they were still sent to the camps. According to the Nazi ideology to not be regarded as Jewish, to be classified as Aryan, one had to go back three or four generations. It was completely crazy!

Do you think visiting Auschwitz is beneficial or advisable for young French people, or high school students?

Yes, but only if they are given some background. Teachers have often told me that they observed profound interest and empathy in their students when they made the pilgrimage to Auschwitz. It was the same for other camps, like the Struthof, in Alsace. But that was only when the visit had taken place after they had heard the testimony of a survivor.

Only a limited number of students should take part in any visit. They must be escorted, not just by a local guide, but ideally by history teachers so the unspeakable can be explained. I especially emphasise that prior to any visit it is vital to have some authentic historical awareness of the genocide of the Jews. It is necessary to point out the specificities of this genocide, unique in the history of humankind. We must also talk to them about the killing of the Romani people, they must not be forgotten in a reckoning of the victims. We also record this memory at the heart of our more general reflections on the barbarity of mankind.

Return to Auschwitz, Forgiveness and Humanism

At a talk given in April 2005, Simone Veil said she thought the younger generation were more sensitive to the memory of the Holocaust than the generations who came immediately after the war. In a way this is a message of optimism, as a real awareness of the horror and the extraordinary nature of this terrible time has developed in the collective consciousness.

Do you think the younger generations reflect and challenge more so than previous generations?

I agree with Simone Veil. There has been a profound change in the current generations compared with the generation immediately after the war.

Firstly, young people today are better informed about what is going on around them and they are often curious about the world. Television and radio keep them in touch, sometimes incessantly, with major events. They are definitely more aware of what has gone on in the past than previous generations. Previous generations were more emotive. Nowadays young people look for explanations about anything they do not understand.

I also feel that civilisation has matured. These days, young people are often very mature at a young age and they are interested in difficult questions.

Will this interest last? Could a general disinterest develop once the last survivors have left us? Will Auschwitz one day just become a nice place for a walk with its flower-lined pathways? This incredible chapter that abandoned humanity, will it then abandon history? I don't know, but it is nice to hope, to keep on teaching in an effort to change humankind for the better.

Of course, I am obviously not talking about all young people. Some young people are completely indifferent to what happened in the Holocaust. Sometimes they clearly show their disinterest in what I am telling them. On the other hand, I have been happily surprised when young people come up to shake my hand and congratulate me. They even encourage me to continue my work of remembrance! So, we must never give up on this generation! Indifference is sometimes just a façade.

I would like to turn to a difficult but important subject, forgiveness. Firstly, one can identify two kinds of forgiveness, the official or public pardon, what we now call 'repentance' in French. The word came into use in a declaration of repentance made by the bishops of France in 1997, with regard to the stance taken by the Church in the face of the persecution of the Jews of France. The word forgiveness can also be reserved for a more private, individual decision on the part of a victim.

Do you think such acts of repentance, which have increased since 1970, are important for survivors? Are they necessary?

For me they are not very important. I even feel such acts of repentance do not apply to me personally.

However, thinking about it, I am sure they are useful. Such actions might affect someone tempted to adopt the same ideology, the same ideas or to repeat such acts of violence. It is also not a bad thing if some people realise that in recent history, the Church, in the broad sense of the word, in a religious or a political sense, has not always taken positions that are consistent with their own ethics. If any acts of repentance can achieve just that, to make some people reassess their blind faith in such authorities, then that is a good thing.

Reading the testimonies of survivors, one can see different reactions towards the perpetrators of these terrible crimes. Some declare their desire for revenge, some a desire for justice and others just don't want to think about their torturers ever again. For many, the crimes committed and the suffering inflicted on victims and their families are unforgiveable. What do you feel about this now? Do you think there are acts that are unforgiveable?

I am going to take from Derrida whose perspective has become mine. If one only forgives what is forgivable, there is no value in that. You are in a kind of pact that has nothing to do with true forgiveness. Yes, there are unforgivable acts, and these are the very acts which should be forgiven.

We must also be careful not to mix it all up – revenge, forgiveness, justice and leniency, among other things. When one reads what has been written by survivors, or even scholars, I often feel there is a lot of confusion in the philosophical sense.

Derrida is a philosopher I feel very close to. He says it is possible to forgive deeds that are unforgivable, but to still bring the perpetrators to justice for their actions. Forgiveness does not necessarily mean leniency. That is something else completely.

Do you think your view has changed over the years? Would you have had the same view immediately after the war or in the years following the war?

I don't know, I don't think about it. I've already told you about my first encounter in Prague a few days before my return to France. When I witnessed the Czech guard beating German prisoners. The unbearable image of that incident remains with me. I could not relate to such violence and revenge. I felt guilty seeing what he did because while he was beating the prisoners he was looking at me as if I had ordered him to do it. So I felt more culpable than vengeful or full of hate when I saw those poor guys suffering with that guard beating them with his belt.

I have always been disgusted by any form of violence. I have always rejected it. That day I was repulsed by what was happening, even though the violence was being meted out to those who represented the perpetrators of my suffering.

So that was my first reaction. I have never felt the need to avenge myself. I have never felt hatred towards the perpetrators of these horrors. I sometimes even understood what they did in the context of their time.

Are the perspectives I have today the result of a slow process of maturity? Maybe. But since that time – even though I was so weak, even though I had only just been freed from the clutches of the SS, even though I still intensely mourned the murder of my parents and my little sister – I still strongly rejected any thoughts of revenge and cruelty. I had no desire, spoken or unspoken, to physically hurt those who were guilty. I felt no relief seeing those German soldiers suffer a beating. In fact it was just the opposite.

What do you think then of people who express hatred as victims or as the family of victims? I remember an interview given by Claude Lanzmann, the director of the film, Shoah. *In the interview, he speaks of his hatred for Suchomel, while he was filming that brute from Treblinka. Can you understand that feeling? An uncontrollable impulse when faced with a criminal who so coldly recounts his zeal for murder with a kind of self-satisfaction, almost cynicism?*

It is really very complex. How can I say how I would have felt if I had ever been in a position like Lanzmann's? What would my reaction have been? I don't know. But if I had felt hatred I would have been sad and very disappointed in myself. Without doubt, we all have a compulsion for aggression, lurking in the depths of our hearts. A compulsion that is looking for the smallest excuse, even a justified one, to reveal itself. Unfortunately we are clearly not only made of love. But when one has known hell on earth, such an experience should foster more wisdom about life and humanity which can be an enriching lesson for oneself and for others.

My first reaction is to feel pity rather than blame for those who remain in a state of hatred. No, I don't blame them, because their suffering endures, suffocating their lives and thwarting their chance of a normal life. Saying this is terrible, but are we not all equal when faced with our hateful compulsion? One day will we be able to manage these feelings? I do not know.

Throughout my own life, I can say I have never had any feelings of hatred. Not just towards the perpetrators of the cruelties I encountered in that place. One cannot go through eighty years of life without coming across people who cause you pain, even in your own family. But I don't hate them.

Perhaps if you don't allow yourself to vent, you can turn back inside yourself or against your family. I have known survivors who reject their own children with real hostility. Some people can repeat the abuse they experienced at the same age with their own children.

As for forgiveness, in my opinion it is a deeply personal thing that is hard to proclaim or make public. It is something you do alone. As I see it, forgiveness is not giving your blessing to the perpetrators of crime. Instead it is being at peace within yourself, not consumed by hatred and having no desire for revenge. It is difficult to generalise so I must emphasise this, I have complete respect for those who cannot forgive.

I would like to read you the thoughts of two survivors of the camps. They look at forgiveness from a similar angle – the unforgiveable and a refusal to forgive.

In Still Alive, *Ruth Klüger wrote, "An injustice is not repaired by the state of mind of the victims of that injustice. I escaped. My life was saved. That is a huge thing. But I did not emerge with a bag full of certificates of acquittal, given to me by the dead, to distribute as I see fit."*

Joseph Bialot, who we have talked about already, wrote, "I detest that well-known saying, 'Forgiven, but not forgotten.' It has the naivety of a boy scout. This pseudo-generosity some people come up with, it offends my ears. To forgive, you first have to forget. If not, every single night the tormentors from the camp will return. Forgive what? Forgive the murder of children? Of old people? Of women? Of thinkers and creators? I say to forget is not possible! Amnesia is not possible!"

What would you say to these survivors if you could speak to them?

I respect what Ruth Klüger says with regard to forgiveness, but why does she allow herself to write with such conviction that a victim's state of mind cannot make amends for the injustices committed?

I refuse to be a victim. I think my position is valid because in my case the oppressors have lost. When Klüger calls forgiveness "... certificates of acquittal, given to me by the dead, to distribute as I see fit," as one would distribute alms, I think she is confusing forgiveness with leniency. To come back to Derrida, I think one can forgive and still bring perpetrators to justice for their crimes. To not bring them to justice would be leniency, not forgiveness.

As for Joseph Bialot, he does not confuse forgiveness with clemency but with forgetting. I do not agree with his assertion that we must forget before we can forgive. To forget is impossible and forgiveness becomes *de facto*. Why put these two concepts together? They are so different and can I dare say to promote this idea is an absurdity. If I could pursue Bialot's idea, that you must forget in order to forgive, when you came to forgive you would have forgotten what you were supposed to forgive! If your soul remains in pain, you will forever remain in the hands of your persecutors.

But doesn't one need time together with genuine work of remembrance and grieving before reaching absolute forgiveness? The philosopher Jankélévitch, in the 1960s, thought that forgiveness was premature after the war. He explained it as a kind of concealment of the crimes. He felt that the genocide of the Jews was being hidden from the collective consciousness, that the perpetrators were quickly going back to a life of comfort in a prosperous Germany, that former French collaborators, many of whom had been granted amnesty in 1951, had won back respectability at such little cost to themselves.

Jankélévitch condemns a false pardon – one that results from simply forgetting, and what he sees as a sign of indifference towards the victims in the years after the war. He confirms that crimes against humanity are not forgivable, and that any "forgiveness was slaughtered in the death camps".

Can the response of some survivors, and a philosopher like Jankélévitch, be explained by an historically legitimate outrage? With regard to the victims, isn't the duty to remember a necessary prerequisite for forgiveness and reconciliation?

You are right. It must be put in context, in the course of history. But despite putting it in its historical context, I do not agree with Jankélévitch at all. I believe there is a kind of confusion here. We just talked about the writers you quoted – on the one hand there is forgiveness, and on the other hand, justice. There is justice and then there is leniency. These are very different concepts. Yes, to get justice criminals must be punished, firstly because they deserve it. They should also be made an example of so the punishment may deter others. Although I have to say, in that area I have few illusions. Justice must be done. However, the course taken by the avengers still seems to me to be dubious.

Does a pardon mean the crime is forgotten? For me, to forgive does not mean to forget.

Furthermore, a group cannot forgive, because forgiveness is an individual thing. Protection from prosecution and unforgiveable acts are also two different concepts. The first is a collective decision while the second is personal and individual. Sure, after our return and until relatively recently, the collective memory ignored these events. In the 1950s, when Jankélévitch was expressing his condemnation, nobody wanted to listen, and such imposed silence was indeed unacceptable. We can look back at the lack of success for Primo Levi's book when it was released in 1947. Though several years later it became a best-seller, selling millions of copies.

So, I would say that forgiveness is possible when remembrance and justice are also possible. That does not mean forgetting or justice being denied.

Jankélévitch includes two further arguments to explain the concept of 'unforgiveable'. For him, forgiveness involves a personal connection between the victim and the perpetrator, something granted willingly. If the victim is no longer here, the crime cannot ever be forgiven as he believes only the victim can pardon the crime. "It is up to the victims to forgive. How can survivors forgive on behalf of all survivors, or in the name of the victims, or in the name of their parents and their families? No, it is not up to us to forgive on behalf of the little children those monsters enjoyed tormenting. The children themselves would have to forgive them." This conclusion is made by many survivors of the death camps. One cannot grant forgiveness by proxy.

He puts forward a second argument also shared by many survivors. He explains that forgiveness assumes some remorse on the part of the perpetrator. It is difficult to grant forgiveness to someone who shows indifference or feels they have done nothing wrong. Someone who has absolutely no remorse. Jankélévitch puts it very clearly, "To qualify for forgiveness, one must confess guilt, unreservedly and without any extenuating circumstances ... Why would we forgive those who do not regret their crimes, not even a little."

Jankélévitch seems to be saying that it is difficult to forgive on behalf of a victim. It is also difficult to forgive someone who remains a monster.

Jankélévitch thinks it is only victims who can forgive, that people cannot forgive on behalf of the martyrs. But can't we identify with the victims? The murder of my father, of my mother, of my little sister – wasn't that my murder as well? To have had that happen to me, doesn't that allow me to identify with the victims?

For example, when Lanzmann says that he feels hatred when he is confronted with a perpetrator of such crimes, he is identifying with the victims and putting himself in their place. He never had to face Suchomel! If he so easily identifies with the victims, can he not understand that others could do the same, not to seek vengeance, but to grant forgiveness? Why accept intellectually that it is possible to identify with the victims only in one sense, that of seeking vengeance, but not when it comes to forgiveness? Our mind allows us to identify with and to feel empathy for the victims.

As for the second proposition from Jankélévitch, I prefer Derrida's position on this point. If the perpetrator seeks forgiveness and feels remorse for the wrong he has committed, you are no longer dealing with the same person. He is no longer the savage. The perpetrator has become another being, a being who is aware of wrongdoing. If you only pardon those who feel remorse and ask to be forgiven, you are no longer pardoning the same perpetrator. That perpetrator no longer exists and your pardon no longer has any value.

It is difficult to see that a perpetrator who has made a confession or claims to be remorseful is radically different from the criminal they were.

It is not the remorse that changes a person, but the fact that they have changed that makes them feel remorse. Of course, I am not talking here of just the word remorse, which we can proclaim just to clear ourselves of some crime. I am talking about a profound inner feeling of repentance.

As we have already discussed, even if they express remorse, we must punish those who have committed acts of barbarity. But we can grant them our forgiveness and still punish them. That is to say, to punish without hatred, and especially without any vengeance which may influence the verdict. Forgiveness is not linked to any verdict. Forgiveness is independent of the culpability or remorse of a perpetrator. After a certain amount of time to process their feelings the victim has nothing to do with the perpetrator. For me, real forgiveness is an extremely personal act, an act for oneself, a gift one grants to oneself. I would go so far as to say that forgiveness should remain discreet and almost unspoken. It should not be shouted from the rooftops.

We should perhaps find a new word for forgiveness. A word that does not depend on the strict definition of an encounter between a victim and a perpetrator, which is an indispensable condition for Jankélévitch, one which also implies a certain strength of feeling. When forgiveness becomes unconditional and unemotional, the act is different and such a difference should surely be part of our language. We really should invent another word for unconditional forgiveness!

In reading some survivors' accounts one can get the impression that enduring the Holocaust has given rise to a particularly pessimistic and tragic view of the human condition. I feel you maintain a position that I would call a belief in humanity 'in spite of everything'. Maybe I can even call you a humanist and an optimist. Is the term 'humanist' meaningful for you? Do you accept it for yourself?

Yes, I accept humanism when defined to mean respect for the dignity of human beings whatever they are like and whatever their situation. You must also see human beings in the context in which they find ourselves, as we have a strong connection to all around us, the animal kingdom, the kingdom of plants, the universe of nature. This is fundamental. Human beings are not independant of the trees which grow around them. Human beings must be placed at the heart of nature and live in harmony with it. Can one love humanity and be disinterested in the environment in which humanity lives – an environment that could disappear if we do not take care of it?

Looking at the modern world as it is evolving, do you think we are more respectful of nature and humanity than in the past? Do you think humanism has progressed or is there a 'crisis for humanism'?

The two go together. Human beings do not seem to be aware of the risks they face if they do not respect nature. In a way they have lost a sense of balance and what is beneficial for humanity. However, at the same time there is an awareness that did not exist before. Some, and in no small measure, realise that life cannot be protected if we do not make a concerted effort to protect nature.

On the one hand, unfortunately, the majority only think of profit, of power, of economic and material success, of an egocentric life. On the other hand, we are aware that we must protect life for the survival of our grandchildren. It is contradictory and complex.

Do you think that human dignity, which is fundamental to your definition of humanism, is more respected today than it was in the past?

Sadly, I must say that the situation is not great and it is getting worse in some places. The rise of totalitarianism, the rise of cults, the rise of religious and political fanaticism, the adoption of radical positions, these all make me feel that humanity is not moving in the right direction at present. Even though there is increasing charitable and humanitarian engagement to help those who suffer in places far away, sadly I feel decision-makers are going in completely the opposite direction.

Your observations are particularly pessimistic and worrying.

Pessimistic, yes, and definitely worrying, but I still have some hope as I think humanity will wake up one day.

And what do you think would make human beings more humane, more respectful of the rights of others? A huge question, obviously.

We must not give up and we must continue working to protect this world. We have a common destiny, to live together, which we can only do if we protect planet earth. If this necessity is not taken seriously, and if the decision-makers do not recognise the fragility of the earth, it will perish. It will not last forever. I have faith that it will soon improve. If I am being pessimistic here with regards to the state of the world, I am not saying this about people in general, as we have exceptional resources.

I will use an example which demonstrates our awareness. I would have laughed if you had told me twenty years ago that we would have rubbish bins of different colours to sort our waste. I would have thought that no-one would ever comply with it. But look at us now, in just a few years it has become the norm, something we do as a matter of course. It shows a great appreciation of the challenges for the environment. In this area international organisations should provide encouragement and guidelines on a global basis.

Today more than ever, we must consider ourselves as citizens of the world. Borders and states seem crazy to me. Nonsensical and selfish. I think we should all be working for a global government which could override national interests and consider everyone as a citizen of the world.

Do you think we have an obligation to work towards universal solidarity in a world that sometimes seems to be moving in the opposite direction?

Return to Auschwitz, Forgiveness and Humanism

Absolutely. It's essential. The more people do not see someone on the other side of the planet as their brother or sister, the more there will be problems. I'd like to tell you about an experiment that was conducted a few years ago in the United States. Someone was offered a million dollars to kill their mother. They refused. They were offered the same amount to kill their brother. Same response. Then the offer was to kill a neighbour. Refusal! Then someone from the neighbourhood. Still the same refusal. This continued until the proposal was (with impunity) to get rid of a little Chinese man on the other side of the world. There was then a moment of hesitation, before the same refusal. It's that moment of hesitation we must confront. Civilisation must tackle this hesitation, which is certainly small, but makes all the difference. It means everything. The day there is not a moment's hesitation we will have won.

One could imagine even more worrying responses! I am thinking of the historian Christopher Browning's book Ordinary Men *in which he studies the testimonies of a reserve battalion of the German police. For several months this battalion murdered tens of thousands of Jews. These were reserve soldiers, quite ordinary men, not fanatic, monstrous Nazis. They were men with children and a professional life who became murderers, obeying orders out of respect for their command and group loyalty. According to this American historian, very few of these soldiers refused or even tried to avoid carrying out their assignments. Here, we are at the very antithesis of civilisation, unable to identify with another as a human being.*

Romain Gary wrote, "The Nazis were human beings, and what was human within them was their inhumanity." Isn't this very intractable inhumanity a challenge to faith in humanity?

The fact that very few men in that battalion refused to murder Jews doesn't surprise me at all. What often destroys the conscience of an individual is the group. People are capable of accepting anything to maintain their allegiance and to avoid being accused of disloyalty to the group. I also believe that the perpetrators were just ordinary men, as Browning called them. However, civilisation can change for the better, it is really only just beginning.

In Oradour-sur-Glane, the SS of the Reich Division locked several hundred civilians in the church and the commander ordered it be set alight with flame throwers. Who was more responsible: the person who started the fire, or the fanatic who gave the order? In my opinion, the ones who are more responsible are the ones who calmly, dispassionately, set fire to the church because they were blindly following an order, no doubt feeling no sense of culpability. They could have refused, since they only acted to carry out an order. Certainly the group is dangerous, it can be led by flawed commanders, but the individual at the heart of the group, who forgets they are a human being, is even more dangerous.

You can also make more optimistic judgements and say that those who refused to carry out such orders showed extraordinary courage, and had an exceptional conscience in the context of such a unique and devastating war.

We could also define humanity in a way that is more supportive. Limits must be established as to what is unjustifiable or abominable, defining what is intolerable to all human beings. A kind of definitive core upon which one could attempt to reach agreement. Does humanism also mean to refuse certain actions?

We should try to find a common core which can be acceptable for all cultures. Respect for the dignity of others would seem to be the indispensable foundation of a life worth living. Education as a means of creating awareness of others, of their value and their differences, can transform people. The role of education is crucial.

When I say education, I am not just talking about schooling. For me, learning principally comes from the parents, they should be models for their children. For example, education is what educators do every day, but not exclusively. The importance of relationships with others should be paramount. How we relate to others is extended by our culture which connects us with others outside of our usual milieu, through cinema and books. We should use everything that can raise awareness.

I would like to come back to an idea you once spoke to me about, the capacity for human beings to change for the better. According to Rousseau, humans, unlike animals, can evolve in a moral sense to imagine a better world and work towards an ideal which allows them to improve themselves. This optimistic concept, that it is possible for human nature to evolve in a positive way, has been questioned by a number of thinkers. For some, history shows us that the idea human beings can improve is completely hypothetical and illusory. With its unprecedented crimes, the twentieth century is surely the perfect example to disprove the hypothesis. Do you think the idea that human beings can change for the better is feasible? Is humankind capable of moral development and has it already developed morally?

I am certain of it. I continue to believe that human beings are better than they seem to be. I think again of those people who threw the bread to us despite being shot at by German soldiers. I think of such acts of selfless kindness. Human beings can be amazing and can develop an almost immediate sense of solidarity with another person. Human beings are evolving creatures who have already transformed significantly since our origins.

Of course genocides have continued to occur since the Holocaust. This causes us to question our faith in humanity. Time has an important role in putting these extremely pessimistic observations into perspective. What is essential is to believe in the capacity of human beings to change for the better. What are a few decades, one or two centuries, in the history of humankind? Not much, just a fleeting moment in time. It shouldn't mean that you become a confirmed pessimist who disregards time and our long history.

For some, I am thinking especially of Imre Kertész, what is surprising is not evil, but goodness, and what he calls the 'irrational' characteristic of goodness. For him evil is typical, goodness is rare.

In Kaddish pour un enfant qui ne naîtra pas [22] *the narrator tells the story of a teacher who got some bread that belonged to another inmate in his camp. The teacher could have easily kept the bread and eaten it without anyone knowing. But instead, he finds the inmate to give the bread to him.*

That freely given gift, absolute proof of altruistic kindness, was hard to explain and shocked the narrator. The exercise of altruistic kindness is a mystery for this Hungarian writer, and you can see where he is coming from. The Righteous were quite rare in France even if they did indeed exist.

For some, like Tzvetan Todorov, the Righteous had particular characteristics. They were resistants or rebels, sometimes on the fringe, and they were people who defied the law. They were not those who displayed the highest moral principles who acted to save a stranger at peril to their own lives. What do you think it is that makes someone more righteous, more compassionate?

That's a very difficult question. Yes, I believe to be a Righteous person you had to be defiant because the laws at that time would not tolerate dissent. But to just defy the law was not enough.

I don't know how one becomes a Righteous person. I only know that there were people, mostly just ordinary people, whose souls

---

22. Translation of title: Prayer of mourning for a child who will not be born.

had not been poisoned by extremist religious or entrenched political beliefs. I still remember a friend who was hidden during the war in a village in the Luberon. The whole village protected him. The Milice came one day and nobody denounced him. I believe, unlike the Protestants (in Chambon-sur-Lignon for example), very few mainstream Catholics hid Jews. Personally, I think the absence of any stance by their leader, the Pope, played an important role in this. On an individual level, some Catholics sheltered and protected Jews, as did some convents. But there was no large-scale effort to support the Jews. If the Pope had taken a more decisive stand, I think more effort would have been made by Catholics to help Jews.

How does one become a Righteous person? By realising you are a human being, that's all. The incredible beauty in feeling like a human being. To just be human, not a hero.

To be a human being, does that mean to feel instant empathy for someone else who is suffering? One looks again at a thinker like Rousseau, for whom pity is one of the basic principles of a humane consciousness. For him, at times a culture can make us forget pity. Scholars do not necessarily develop a superior moral conscience. Many, instead of pity, have love of self and individual interests. In any case, Rousseau reminds us there is no link between the level of sophistication of a culture and the exercise of altruistic pity or empathy for others.

Absolutely! Again we must define what culture is. Culture should not separate human beings from the rest of the world and from other human beings. Culture includes the humanity of humankind. It is different from learning, which accumulates knowledge without concern for the future of human beings and their progress.

In conclusion, I would like to offer a perspective from a contemporary psychoanalyst, Nathalie Zaltzman. She has reflected deeply on the experience of the camps and on the death wish. On the one hand, she says humanism has its limits, and it is impossible to completely control the death wish and the compulsion for aggression in human beings. On the other hand, she explains, we must have faith in this culture and the reasoning we do have, which also defines us as human beings. Because these are the only things we have to curb the destructive urges within ourselves. "History has shown that culture and reasoning do not have the capacity to have a direct impact on curbing the death wish in human beings. However, these are the only things that give us the strength to not surrender to the death wish."

I completely agree with that conclusion. Nevertheless, we have no choice. We either kill ourselves with irrational pessimism, or conversely, we accept living with happiness and having faith that human beings can change for the better. That is the meaning I give to knowledge and culture. This effort to relate to the 'other', with other human beings, to counter suspicion and death. That is my challenge as a humanist.

Translator's Note

In 2007 I visited the Shoah Memorial in Paris and saw a profoundly moving exhibition *Les Justes de France* (The Righteous of France), dedicated to those who risked their lives to save Jewish people in France during the Holocaust.

A decade later, I met a French expatriate living in Melbourne, Valérie Katz, who shared my interest in the experience of French Jews during World War II. She introduced me to a book featuring the testimony of Holocaust survivor Sam Braun, *Personne ne m'aurait cru, alors je me suis tu* and a website www.lesenfantsdesam.fr created by Sam's family to continue his educational work.

Inspired, I contacted Sam's family who warmly welcomed my offer to translate their website into English. Then I turned my attention to translating Sam's book. On completing the English manuscript, I needed a publisher and, through a series of lectures organised by the Jewish Holocaust Centre in Melbourne, I discovered Real Publishing who embraced the opportunity to make this book a reality.

Sam's daughter Malka Braun once told me that her late papa would be so happy looking down upon us in this endeavour. I have also felt Sam's guiding hand in the many moments of serendipity I have experienced along the way—meeting Valérie, receiving the unreserved support of Malka and her mother Beatrice, and being granted the translation rights from the book's French publisher

Albin Michel gratis – all of which will enable me to donate this English version of Sam's book to Holocaust museums and libraries across the world.

My hope is that, through this translated publication, Sam Braun's work of remembrance and his words of humanity, kindness, and forgiveness will continue to resonate.

Victoria Taylor
Melbourne, Australia
2022

References

As found in the French edition, *Personne ne m'aurait cru, alors je me suis tu*, Albin Michel, 2008

Antelme (Robert), *L'Espèce humaine*, Gallimard, 1999.

Appelfeld (Aharon), *Tsili*, Le Seuil, 2004.

Appelfeld (Aharon), *Histoire d'une vie*, Éditions de l'Olivier, 2004.

Arendt (Hannah), *Condition de l'homme moderne*, Calmann-Lévy, 1994.

Arendt (Hannah), *Eichmann à Jérusalem*, Gallimard, 1997.

Bensoussan (Georges), *Auschwitz en héritage ? Du bon usage de la mémoire*, Mille et une nuits 2003.

Bialot (Joseph), *C'est en hiver que les jours rallongent*, Le Seuil, 2002.

Billet (Marie), *À l'ombre des Justes*, Elytis, 2007.

Borowski (Tadeusz), *Le Monde de pierre*, Christian Bourgois, 2002.

Browning (Christopher), *Des hommes ordinaires*, Les Belles Lettres, 2005.

Camus (Albert), *Le Premier Homme*, Gallimard, 1994.

Delbo (Charlotte), *Auschwitz et après* (3 tomes), Éditions de Minuit, 1970, 1971.

Delbo (Charlotte), *La Mémoire et les Jours*, Berg International, 1991.

Derrida (Jacques), *Le Pardon*, Descartes et Cie, 2006.

Didi-Huberman (Georges), *Images malgré tout*, Éditions de Minuit, 2003.

Faye (Jean-Pierre) et Vilaine (Anne-Marie de), *La Déraison antisémite et son langage*, Actes Sud, 1993.

Gary (Romain), *Les Cerfs-volants*, Gallimard, 1983.

Gilbert (Martin), *Les Justes. Les héros méconnus de la Shoah*, Calmann-Lévy, 2004.

Hilberg (Raul), *Exécuteurs, victimes, témoins : la catastrophe juive, 1933-1945*, Gallimard, 2004.

Horkheimer (Max), *Notes critiques pour le temps présent*, Payot 1993.

Jankélévitch (Vladimir), *L'Imprescriptible*, Le Seuil, 1996.

Kertész (Imre), *Être sans destin*, Actes Sud, 1998.

Kertész (Imre), *Kaddish pour un enfant qui ne naîtra pas*, Actes Sud, 1995.

Klarsfeld (Serge), *Vichy-Auschwitz. La « solution finale » et la question juive en France*, Fayard, 1983 et 1985.

Klüger (Ruth), *Refus de témoigner*, Viviane Hamy, 1997.

Lazare (Julien), *Le Livre des Justes*, Jean-Claude Lattès, 1993.

Levi (Primo), *Si c'est un homme*, Buchet-Chastel, 1961 (Se questo è un uomo, Da Silva, 1947).

Levi (Primo), *Les Naufragés et les Rescapés*, Gallimard, 1989.

Levi (Primo), *Conversations et entretiens*, Robert Lafont, 1998.

Moscovici (Jean-Claude), *Voyage à Pitchipoï*, L'École des loisirs, 1995.

Nissim (Gabriele), *Le Jardin des Justes*, Éditions Payot & Rivages, 2007.

Ricœur (Paul), *La Mémoire, l'histoire, l'oubli*, Le Seuil, 2000.

Rousseau (Jean-Jacques), *Discours sur l'origine et les fondements de l'inégalité parmi les hommes, précédé du Discours sur les sciences et les arts*, LGF, 1996.

Semprun (Jorge), *Le Grand Voyage*, Gallimard, 1991.

Semprun (Jorge), *L'Écriture ou la vie*, Gallimard, 1996.

Sereny (Gitta), *Au fond des ténèbres*, Denoël, 1975.

Stern (Mario Rigoni), *Le Poète secret*, La Fosse aux Ours, 2005.

Tillion (Germaine), *À la recherche du vrai et du juste*, Le Seuil, 2001.

Todorov (Tzvetan), *Mémoire du mal, tentation du bien*, Robert Laffont, 2000

Todorov (Tzvetan), *Face à l'extrême*, Le Seuil, 1994.

Vernant (Jean-Pierre), « Histoire de la mémoire et mémoire historienne », dans *Œuvres. Réligions, Rationalités, Politique*, Le Seuil, 2007, t. II.

Vidal-Naquet (Pierre), *Les Assassins de la mémoire*, Le Seuil, 1995.

Weintrater (Régine), *Sortir du génocide*, Payot, 2003.

Zaltzman (Nathalie), *De la guérison psychanalytique*, PUF, 1998.

www.ingramcontent.com/pod-product-compliance
Lightning Source LLC
Chambersburg PA
CBHW051436290426
44109CB00016B/1579